REVOLUTION IS FOR US

First published 2013 by Interventions Publishing
Republished 2019 by Interventions Inc

Interventions is a not-for-profit, independent left wing book publisher. For further information:
www.interventions.org.au
interventionspublications@gmail.com
Trades Hall Suite 68
54 Victoria Street
Carlton VIC 3053

Cover photo: The first open Gay Liberation contingent, International Women's Day, Sydney, 11 March 1972

Typeset in Adobe Caslon Pro by Les Thomas
Original cover design by Les Thomas
New cover design by Viktoria Ivanova,

Author: Ross, Liz
Title: Revolution is for Us: The Left and Gay Liberation in Australia

ISBN: 978-0-646-90179-4 : Paperback

©Liz Ross 2013
The moral rights of the author have been asserted
All rights reserved. Except where permitted by Australian copyright law, no part of this book may be transmitted or reproduced in any form by any means without permission in writing from the publisher.
All inquiries should be made to the author.

A catalogue record for this book is available from the National Library of Australia

Revolution is for Us

The Left and Gay Liberation
in Australia

Liz Ross

INTERVENTIONS
MELBOURNE

*Dedicated to all those who have fought for liberation.
For the fighters of the future, for those in whose time
revolution will come.*

Contents

Acknowledgements vi
Introduction vii

Chapter 1
LOVE'S COMING OF AGE 1

Chapter 2
DESIRE, SHAME AND REBELLION 18

Chapter 3
GENERATION ON FIRE. THE SIXTIES 37

Chapter 4
GAY LIBERATION. THE AGE OF DEMONSTRATIONS 56

    THE TURN TO RADICAL FEMINISM 69

Chapter 5
GAY LIBERATION. THE ROAD TO MARDI GRAS ...72

Chapter 6
RED AND LAVENDER 91

    THE BATTLE OF IDEAS 105

Chapter 7
REVOLUTION IS FOR US! 117

Endnotes 119
Bibliography 137

Acknowledgements

I want to thank all those who gave so generously of their time for interviews. I also want to mention Bill Leslie and Naomi Cranenburgh, both of whom died before the book was finished and whose research and activism made valuable contributions.

My special thanks go to Gary Jaynes for his friendship, unfailing patience and help during my many hours of research at ALGA. The book would not have been possible without the resources of the Australian Gay and Lesbian Archives and all those who have kept the Archives going.

Thanks to Les Thomas for the original greatcover and book design. Also thanks to Viktoria Ivanova for the great new cover. I also thank all my comrades in Socialist Alternative who have encouraged me and provided the stimulating debates, discussion and revolutionary practice that have provided the political frame-work for this book.

Revolution is for Us is so much the better for the invaluable con-tribution from Tom O'Lincoln, who has so generously given of his time and political knowledge and understanding. A challeng-ing editor – just the sort you need to have!

I acknowledge the valued support of the Jeff Goldhar Project.

Thanks to Peter Murphy and the Search Foundation for the generous financial support, despite differences over some of my analysis of the CPA.

Finally, I acknowledge the valued support of Interventions Inc in producing this second printing.

INTRODUCTION

"The homosexual is essential to the sexual revolution; there can be no revolution, no liberation, without us." Or so Australia's Gay Liberation wrote about the future revolution in one of its earliest leaflets.[1]

Gay Liberation was the last of the liberation movements to appear in Australia. Its politics and practice drew on those of the Black and Women's movements and the Left. Its vibrant history is still being written, with much that lay hidden (or forgotten) being uncovered by a younger generation of lesbian and gay historians, as well as by those who were there.

This history focusses on the left wing politics of the Australian Gay Liberation Movement, including detailing some of the earlier Australian history of the left and sexuality by way of setting the scene for the explosion of activism from the early 1970s. In *Revolution is for Us* the CPA stands out as the major left wing force. Much of it could almost be called a history of the Communist Party because of the significant role it played from the 1920s to the 1980s. The party attracted many militants and was the instigator or a leading participant in a wide range of struggles. It is, despite the distortions of Stalinism and the impact of the Depression, World Wars and the Cold War, a largely positive history.

The book offers a history of the early militant fight for gay rights, finishing with the highpoint of the 1978 Mardi Gras. It is a new history in that it describes the story of Gay Liberation and the fight for gay rights in Australia explicitly from the perspective of the left.

Left-wing involvement in Gay Liberation has been ignored or more often distorted, often referring only at those groups which were hostile to gay liberation. Aubrey Walter claims that "indeed most of the traditional left organisations initially saw homosexuals as mere 'decadent excrescences' on the body politic".[2] The close involvement of left groups in Gay Liberation itself, in the campaigns, conferences and action on the streets, during the hey-day of the fight for gay liberation have generally been sidelined. It is not just modern history where the role of the left has been obscured. The earlier history of the German Social Democratic Party's open support for gay rights, including attempts to remove anti-homosexual laws, as well as the Russian Revolution's sweeping reforms are only mentioned by the far left.

Rather than directly refute every distortion and correct every omission, I will instead outline what role the left did play. I do not argue that everyone – or even a majority of gay activists – were Marxists, in fact very few were. I point to the influential role of Marxist ideas and left-wing activists in the movement. Gay Liberation was a movement born in a time when "revolution was in the air", when the Marxist ideas of oppression, exploitation and liberation were common currency. The early GLF welcomed this left analysis, using it to inform its strategies and tactics. However as the revolutionary tide ebbed, other analyses based on patriarchy theory and leading to separatist strategies gained currency. Nonetheless, some kept the ideas of socialism alive in the movement, leaving a legacy for later lesbian and gay activists to draw on. It is this story that is told here.

The story unfolds...

"Love's coming of age", Chapter One, begins the history with a brief look at some early socialist groups and then to the foundation days of the Communist Party of Australia in 1920. It continues in a broad sweep from the early days until 1971, when that same party became the first to raise the issue of gay liberation in its weekly paper, *Tribune*. "Desire, shame and rebellion", Chapter Two, looks more closely at the 1950s and casts a somewhat different light on that period than the commonly-held notions of a repressive, anti-sex, "white picket fence" society. Repression, as Marilyn Lake points out, was only necessary because of the "desire" and "rebellion" that was some of the legacy of the years of Depression and war.[3]

"Generation on fire - the sixties", Chapter Three, describes that quintessential decade of revolt, detailing the rise of the struggle for homosexual rights which exploded onto the streets of New York in 1969 with the Stonewall riots. It also looks at the earliest, pioneering organisations of homosexuals in America and Australia. In Australia it took the events of the late 60s to inspire the formation of the new groups, which in a few short months, condensed the decades of experience of overseas "homophile" groups.

Gay Liberation first appeared in Australia at the end of 1971 and the next two chapters Gay Liberation. The age of demonstrations", Chapter Four and "Gay Liberation. The road to Mardi Gras", Chapter Five, detail the two exciting phases of Gay Liberation, which ended with the 1978 Mardi Gras.

At the end of Chapter Four and in Chapter Six there are separate sections dealing with some theoretical questions that arose in the movement's history.

"Red and Lavender", Chapter Six, counters the histories that deny a place to the organised Left's key role in fighting for lesbian and gay liberation. Rather than focus on the groups that were hostile to, and played next to no role in the movement, I detail the actual history of the Communist Party of Australia, the Socialist Workers Party and the International Socialists in Gay Liberation and the many campaigns, conferences, events up to the Mardi Gras.

The final chapter, "Revolution is for us", sums up the critical role of the left in the fight for gay liberation.

CHAPTER 1

Love's Coming of Age[1]

Praise flowed for Edward Carpenter's *Love's Coming of Age*, a book whose mission was "to remove the altar of love from present dens of stuffy upholstery to the high canopy of the stars."[2]

This praise came from none other than Victorian Socialist Party firebrand John Curtin, in that year of revolution, 1917. Curtin had just moved to Perth to spread socialist politics in the West, and to edit the *Westralian Worker*. Although never confirmed, it seems Curtin also took over the role of the paper's book reviewer, giving himself the name of Vigilant.

Vigilant thought the time was right to "grasp firmly the nettle of social evils and particularly the immediate moment with its surfeit of sex-problem picture shows ... to direct public attention to some really serious works upon the subject ... *Love's Coming of Age* deals with the sex-problem in its every aspect."

While it's not entirely clear what the sex-problem was, Vigilant argued strongly "that the only ultimate complete solution of the sex-problem, bound up as it is with the economic dependence of woman, lies in the emancipation of society. This idea comes naturally to Socialists, who understand the nature of the economic serfdom of today and who cleave to the classic statement [by Engels]: 'Never shall this problem be solved until there lives upon this earth a race of youths and maidens who have never been obliged, nor even tempted, to enter a loveless match, nor deterred from entering a love match, through material motives – considerations of social prestige on the one hand, or the necessity for a home on the other'."

The book was definitely challenging, with "daring tentative suggestions" which would probably prevent young people being allowed to read it. But Vigilant was having none of this, seeing it as suitable for adolescents, while adding that "its sweet ideals" should be passed on by parents to their children, so that "when their turn comes, they may approach the enchanted lands of love and marriage with fuller knowledge". Although these "daring tentative suggestions" must have included Carpenter's chapter on homosexuality – the Intermediate Sex as he called it – Vigilant never directly refers to homosexuality. In a later issue Vigilant writes about Oscar Wilde, praising him for writing "some of the finest moral essays in the English language", but notes that his name "is with rough-minded men a by-word for perverted crime".[3]

Ross's Monthly of that same year wasn't so coy. With its masthead proclaiming a magazine of "Protest, Personality and Progress. A racy newspaper – racy of the soil. (earthy)", it's not surprising *Ross's* tackled some of the "hot-button" topics of the day. Heading the review of *Love's Coming of Age*, "A courageous sex book", it wrote of "a very illuminating chapter on *The Intermediate Sex*". Further study, said the magazine, would lead to a considerable modification of views on the subject of marriage and sex relations. From this, the reviewer noted, Carpenter moved naturally to discussion of a possible Free Society.[4]

"A compelling issue" – the early socialists

Sex, including homosexuality, was – and has continued to be – a compelling issue for the left. Other writers also have pointed to the rise of lesbian and gay rights in tandem with revolutions. One of the first examples is the French Revolution of 1791 resulting in the effective decriminalisation of homosexuality. The Napoleonic Code of 1804, based on the ideals of the Revolution, was widely adopted throughout Europe. Equally influential was the Russian Revolution of 1917, with its sweeping changes affecting all aspects of life including the decriminalisation of homosexuality. In 1920, a leading young Bolshevik David Khanin extolled the expressions of love. "In the name of revolution did we suppress in ourselves explosions of feelings and the flesh? No, a thousand times, no! We loved just as other generations..." Historian Gregory Carleton wrote of the times that, "People could not remain silent in the midst of a revolution which was the most audacious effort in history" to free people to love as they chose and put an end to prejudice.[5]

1917 also inspired socialists in Australia. Victorian Socialist Party (VSP) member Amelia Lambrick observed "a time of rapid movement. Old methods, old ideas, old conceptions are in the crucible. Changes vital and far reaching are making themselves felt."[6] One of those changes was the formation of a new, revolutionary party. On 26 October 1920, twenty-six women and men from socialist groups, the Industrial Workers of the World (IWW) and some unionists from the NSW 'Trades Hall Reds' current met in Sydney to form the Communist Party of Australia (CPA)[7]. A party which explicitly aligned itself with the Russian Revolution and saw itself as a dedicated activist revolutionary party.

The original manifesto insisted that the Communist Party was a fighting organisation and not a debating club. Adds Stuart Macintyre, "The success of the Bolsheviks was taken to validate Lenin's insistence on the need to seize the revolutionary opportunity; the split in the ranks of the pre-war socialist international was seen as distinguishing those who made revolution, from those who merely talked of one."[8] With the working class the agents of change in Russia, the CPA's overwhelming orientation was to this class. That approach led to significant differences between the new Communist Party and existing socialist groups such as the VSP, even though some from the Victorian Socialists had been part of the CPA's first gathering.[9]

However as the fledgling workers' state faced famine, war and the decimation of the working class, the political situation in Russia deteriorated. From the early 1920s Joseph Stalin began his rise to power. Ruthlessly destroying the revolution's political gains, Stalin transformed Russia into a state capitalist power.[10] The challenges to prejudice and restriction of the early days came under attack as the

Stalinist regime vigorously promoted the capitalist nuclear family, tighter divorce laws, restrictions on abortion and in March 1934, the re-criminalisation of homosexuality.

Leon Trotsky, one of the Revolution's leaders, was a fierce opponent of Stalin and the degeneration in Russia. Particularly scathing of Stalin's valorisation of the family, Trotsky charged that: "the leaders are forcing people to glue together again the shell of the broken family...to consider it, under the threat of extreme penalties, the sacred nucleus of triumphant socialism. It is hard to measure... the scope of this retreat."[11] Portrayed by Stalin as an enemy of the revolution, he became a hated figure in the Stalinised Communist Parties. Nonetheless Trotsky's influence was not completely lost. Exiled from Russia, he called for the formation of revolutionary political groups around the world to carry on the Bolshevik tradition he'd been so much a part of establishing. Some heeded his call, forming "Trotskyist" groups around the world, including in Australia. But the group here was too small to be influential and it is to the other socialist groups, the VSP and the CPA, that we turn to for the history of the left and sexuality up to the sixties.

The VSP, one of Australia's first socialist groups illustrates some of the early response to the issues of sex and sexuality.[12] In the VSP, for all its focus on relations between the sexes and other social questions, homosexuality only appeared in an indirect way in book reviews in the pages of their publications. There was no call for ending the criminalisation of homosexual behaviour or other proposals for change. In contrast, in the mainstream press of its time (1905-1923), there were regular mentions of men charged with a variety of homosexual crimes, some on women who cross-dressed or even married other women, a few about lesbians and an article on a "remarkable theory" of homosexuality.[13]

Edward Carpenter's first mention in the VSP's weekly paper *The Socialist* was a letter from him weighing in on the debate within the socialist movement around the question of general strikes. While selections from Oscar Wilde's *Ballad of Reading Jail* were published and the American radical poet Walt Whitman was praised for his working class verses, again no mention was made of either man's homosexuality or homosexual references in their works.[14]

Once *The Socialist* did respond to the mainstream press coverage. 'Passing women', women who dress and live as men, have occurred throughout history and in Australia, often during times of high unemployment. There have been a number of high profile cases, one of which was Marion (Bill) Edwards. In 1906 *The Socialist* put her case as a strong argument for equal pay, rather than anything to do with sexuality. As the paper wrote: "Marion Edwards who had been dressing in male attire for the last seven years is a Welsh girl. She says she first donned male clothes to enable her to get a living easier than she could as one of the gentler sex. Moral – equal pay for equal work and thorough training for both sexes, with economic freedom for all."[15]

From the beginning, in the socialist and communist press books were routinely recommended for reading, including many about 'sex hygiene' and education. Havelock Ellis's *Men and Women*, Carpenter's *Love's coming of age*, Richard von Krafft-Ebbing's *Psychopathia Sexualis*, along with Oscar Wilde's *The soul of socialism* and *Collected Works*, were merely noted as a books for sale with no further comment or review. *The Socialist*, however, did refer readers to *Ross's Monthly* – where readers could find Carpenter's "brave book", among other detailed reviews.

The book that is key to Marxist sexual politics, Frederick Engels' *Origin of the family, private property and the state* was regularly referred to. There were frequent extracts and many articles based on the book, all a mark of how seriously the VSP took the question. August Bebel's *Women and Socialism*, Eleanor Marx Aveling and Edward Aveling's *The woman question* and outspoken Bolshevik Alexandra Kollontai's books were also frequently referred to, with extracts printed in the paper's columns.

If women become rebels

How did the newly formed CPA respond to issues of sex and sexuality? Was it a champion of sexual freedom or did its practice more closely match critic Eric Hobsbawm's portrayal of post-revolutionary Russia as repressive, puritanical and with "a paralysing fear of love and eroticism"?[16]

Sexuality in the early socialist and communist press primarily came up in five contexts: marriage, birth control, prostitution, sexually transmitted diseases and censorship. In dealing with sexual questions in a positive light, the socialists were in advance of society. However, there can be no denying that such discussions did not reach the heights of the Russian Revolution. Nor did the party propose legislation similar to the Napoleonic Code in place in some European states. Homosexuality was rarely mentioned. Where it did appear it was mostly associated with right-wing figures or was viewed negatively until the 1950s when more neutral references were made.

Nonetheless, having come from a political environment where socialists did address questions of sexuality, the CPA initially didn't shy away from covering such issues in its publications. On the front page of the first edition of their paper *The Communist*, the party published Adela Pankhurst's "Communism and social purity: An appeal to women." Pankhurst predicted that if the Party ever became a force large enough to be feared by the capitalist class, "we shall be associated in the press by accusations of 'Free Love' and 'Communism of Women'." [17]

Pankhurst turned such accusations back on the capitalist class, arguing that "profits and prostitution – upon these Empires are built and Kingdoms stand." Instead, though putting it somewhat more conservatively than the Russians envisaged, she argued, "Communism will abolish prostitution . . . it will encourage purity and decent self-restraint. It will give young men and women the opportunity of marriage based on mutual love, because it will remove poverty and drudgery out of the lives of everyone."

Although the article did explain how "capitalism degraded sexuality and forced women into prostitution", it was more moralistic than revolutionary.[18] Later articles in the paper were more progressive. Ella Morgan, for example, argued that communism would mean "the very taste of life" for women and "if women become rebels, the revolution is in sight".[19]

From its beginnings in 1920 the Communist Party took up the cause of women's freedom. Its publications promoted the gains of the revolution for women in Soviet Russia and pointed to what could be won in Australia. International Women's Day – the initiative of German Communist Clara Zetkin – was featured, with regular articles about its history and celebration around the world. Local issues such as the fight for Equal Pay, matching the party's emphasis on working class women, were also covered. The Party's publications carried references to and extracts from all the books mentioned above, as well as selling important texts. In 1921, just a year after the Party's formation, *The Communist* reported the sale of 21 copies of Kollontai's *Communism and the Family* at the Kurri Kurri coalfields in NSW.

With the defeat of the Russian Revolution, however, alongside the defeats of revolutionary uprisings in Europe, the CPA came to embody, as Phil Griffiths argues, a "profound contradiction". The CPA was way out in front of the rest of society on the question of women and other oppressed groups, but the heavy hand of Stalinism led them in a socially conservative direction.[20]

On the one hand, like the Communist Parties around the world, the Australian party ceased to be revolutionary. Heavily influenced by Soviet social conservatism under Stalin's rule, mirroring that of the Anglo-western capitalism, the Party failed to take up the cause of many of the minority groups such as homosexuals. Stuart Mcintyre notes that in the CPA, "Kollontai's emphasis on sexual liberation gave way to Clara Zetkin's interview with Lenin [where Lenin is described as arguing against Zetkin's more permissive attitudes]". The CPA central committee" sent out a circular, drawing attention to Lenin's rebuke...and warned against 'loose practices'." Leader JB Miles repeated the warning at the Eleventh Congress in 1935: "Bolshevism demands a steel-like character and that has to apply on sex questions as well as on other questions."[21]

It was a retrograde step as Joy Damousi writes, "The party Edna Ryan had known at the beginning of the 1930s, one in which sexual freedom was practised and a drag queen was welcome as a member, gave way one in which any leading member had to consult the central committee before entering or leaving a relationship."[22]

On the other hand, however, in many other ways the Party was still well in advance of society's mores. In the face of mass media glorification of women's role in the home, for example, the CPA championed the cause of women at work. While *The Age* editorialised that "the glamour of wage earning is tinsel" and that women's significant work was in family life, the 1925 Party Conference endorsed the industrial program of left wing unionists for a "six pound minimum wage irrespective of sex, six hour day, union preference, child maintenance and motherhood endowment". During the life of the CPA, issues such as birth control, marriage and prostitution were considered to be socialist concerns of importance for *all* workers, and the party covered these issues regularly in its publications and at meetings.

The Communist Party tried on numerous occasions to boost its female membership, but the number of women members remained stubbornly low, a common problem for almost every political organisation. Structural reasons such as lack of child care, double burden of work and housework, on top of women's socialisation undoubtedly contributed. Nonetheless women sometimes had an impact beyond their numbers as a 1925 report from the Melbourne branch noted: "the only section with any fight in them is the women. They beat the men in Melbourne by miles. One of these women is worth a hundred of these arm-chair philosophers." [23]

In contrast to the party's stance on homosexuals, the CPA's principled and active support for Aboriginal rights shows what the party was capable of on the question of minorities. Some of the difference between the party's stance on Indigenous Australians and homosexuals can be put down to a lack of homosexuals organising for their own rights as compared to the Indigenous community's activism. However, until the late 1960s even where there was some union support, particularly from the Teachers Union, for gay workers victimised or discriminated against, there was no overt CPA backing. There was one notable attempt to organise for law reform by homosexuals. In 1958 Laurie Collinson – CPA member, homosexual and poet – attempted to set up a homosexual law reform group. Although privately a number of homosexuals and heterosexuals were supportive, none were prepared to go public and the group folded.[24]

One of the Communist Party's more progressive campaigns was against censorship.

Australian censors prided themselves on their vigilance in protecting "the Empire's moral core" and being the "bulwark of Anglo-Saxon values"; critics such as author Nettie Palmer countered with the description of censorship as "the fog on our wharves".[25] Publications could be restricted by Customs, the police, the postal service and the Minister, with the grounds for censorship equally numerous. In 1921, in an effort to prevent American comics circulating, the Federal Government issued a proclamation banning many overseas publications. An unexpected result was the flowering of a local writing and publishing, including locally-based comics.[26] Obscenity and sedition laws were strengthened and CPA publications were regularly denied permission to be sent through the post.[27]

Book listings in CPA papers always included a range of publications on questions such as birth control, because as Joy Damousi points out, issues related to sex hygiene and sexology were "part of the modern, rationalist project [of socialism]". *Working Woman* also published selections from Alexandra Kollontai's *Communism and the Family*, which argued that the emancipation of women from economic dependence on men would liberalise marriage and free women in their family and personal lives.[28]

Left wing books such as Kollontai's regularly faced the censor's ban; and the frequent charges of obscenity for political books, left-wing literature and even scientific texts, drew the Party into a more broad-ranging protest against censorship. It wasn't just overseas books and films that were proscribed, a number of novels and plays written or performed by Party members also attracted the censors' scrutiny – and the Party's active defence. In the mid-1920s NSW Labor Premier Jack Lang tried to ban *Workers Weekly* and other working class literature from Sydney's Domain, bringing on determined resistance backed by the NSW Trades and Labour Council.

The Crimes Act was also aimed directly at the activities of the Party, unions and the IWW. The 1920s persecution culminated in raids of Party premises and the printing press in 1929. At the same time, somewhat contradictorily, the authorities eased up other criminal penalties, including those for male homosexual sex, which were halved in 1924.

Despite the censorship drive, the beginning of the 1920s was so inspirational, so hopeful for coming world-wide workers revolutions; there was also a certain freeing up of society's strictures. The 1920s "New Woman" went to university, becoming doctors and engineers, some were adventurers on land and in the new flying machines; or were like Alice Anderson who ran her own garage with an all-female staff in Kew.[29] As Melbourne's most famous lesbian, Monte Punshon, recalled, it was "an exciting time in which to come of age as a woman – a time which seemed to hold great promise".[30]

Dark days and challenges

But by the end of the decade there was financial catastrophe, the defeat of both the 1923 German revolution and the workers uprisings in Italy, with the subsequent rise of fascism. With Stalin and his supporters entrenched in Russia, repression rather than freedom became the order of the day.

The situation worsened in the 1930s. Alongside the workers movement, socialist and communist groups and Jews, homosexuals and their organisations were targeted by rising right-wing forces. In Germany, where the biggest homosexual rights organisation existed, the Nazis quickly turned on them, destroying their headquarters and sending many to concentration camps and murdering or driving into exile most of the activists. This was an incalculable blow to the campaign for homosexual rights world-wide.

In Australia the police shut down CPA meetings and banned John Reed's *Ten Days that Shook the World*, his account of the Russian Revolution. In 1931, after changes to the Crimes Act that virtually made the CPA illegal, Tom Devanny a leading NSW member was arrested, then convicted,[31] During the early 30s he was regularly arrested and convicted, while another member, Beatrice Taylor was suspended from the Education Department in 1933 for teaching the Russian Revolution. Nonetheless, out of the traumas and repression of the 1930s the CPA grew, reaching a high point of 20,000 by 1942. The period also saw a flowering of the Party's cultural activities, especially amongst women members. Writers such as Jean Devanny undertook a serious studies of human relationships in her book *Sex Life of Peoples Ancient and Modern*. She and Katharine Susannah Prichard wrote challenging depictions of women (and men) as workers, mothers, lovers, wives, as well as raising the socially controversial topics of birth control and abortion.

Writing later about the post-WWI period Devanny described a time of change and hope for a better world. Initially "the whole stream of our sexual life today is tending to become debased, tainted, rotten at its source, because our rigid marriage code will not bend to the new demands of it …The system was in a state of flux, of hopeless muddle and the people's social and sex life had to follow suit." But the Russian Revolution provided new hope, she thought, while WWI itself had delivered a stunning blow to monogamous marriage and changed views on illegitimacy such that it would never again be seen as shameful.[32]

Homosexuals are sympathetically portrayed in a number of novels by CPA members, though none of the Party's reviews mentioned these characters. Christina Stead's 1934 novel *Seven Poor Men of Sydney* sets one scene at a well-known homosexual beat at The Gap.[33] In Stead's *Letty Fox, Her Luck*, as well as Devanny's *Virtuous Courtesan*, there are lesbian and male homosexual characters. Appearing in the late 20s, *Virtuous Courtesan* unlike most of Devanny's material, was published in the US with few copies reaching Australia. The authorities banned it anyway and it was one of the few Devanny books not reviewed by *Workers Weekly*.[34] The stage also attracted Party members who embraced a slogan attributed to Lenin that "Art is a weapon", forming the Workers Art Club which became the New Theatre.[35] Plays and novels frequently sparked a spirited debate within the party, with reviews and commentary published in *Tribune*.

Prominent party women such as Joy Barrington and Jean Devanny gained a reputation as firebrands, undaunted by repeated arrests and convictions. And as Stuart Macintyre argues, the party attracted new people, many of them artists. "For many of the creative younger generation who came to adulthood during the decade, witnessed the collapse of the old society and felt the dangers of fascism and war, communism seemed the only realistic alternative. Even those who did not submit to the demands of party membership were drawn into its ambience of cultural engagement."[36]

Repression did, of course, have an impact. While opposing censorship, during the 1950s the party sometimes veered towards a nationalist and moralistic stance on comics, in particular those from the US. Describing the latter, often correctly, as anti-women, violent and pro-imperialist, *Tribune* argued instead for supporting local publications and writers and the supposedly more wholesome Australian comics. Overall, however, the CPA during that time took a dim view of all comics as a corrupting influence on young people and supported the Queensland Trades and Labour Council's campaign to "rid Australia of such filth".[37] On the question of homosexuality, the party's initial response was negative too.[38] The first explicit mention of homosexuality in Communist Party press was a reference to Nazi "excesses", the view of homosexuality as a fascist perversion. On 29 June 1937 *Workers Weekly*, commented that while the Nazi press trumpeted the news of "sexual aberrations" committed by Catholic priests, they said nothing about their own "sexual excesses". *Workers Weekly's* article exposed the cases of two Nazis, the Mayor of Grenzach and a politician in Pforzheim who had been convicted of homosexuality and a Nazi teacher's child abuse. The next post was on 24 June, 1943. The Queensland leader of the Australian Workers Union had penned an attack on the CPA and in reply *Tribune* accused him of plagiarising material from the "moral pervert, fraud and faker...Gestapo spy", Jan Valtin.

There was nothing for ten years, then on 1 July *Tribune* reported a book-burning by officials at US Consulates in Sydney and Singapore. It began: 'If you want to buy 'Why Men Wear Female Clothing' or 'Private Letters from Homosexuals to a Doctor' you can walk into any American bookstore and plunk down your 35 cents. But if you want to read Einstein's Theory of Relativity, Longfellow's epic poem Hiawatha, Mark Twain's Tom Sawyer... and many of the enduring classics, you have to hurry to the nearest incinerator – because that's where they are today."[39] Hardly the most positive of references. Another 1953 article listed Joseph Mazzell, "earlier convicted of adultery and sodomy" as testifying against the jailed US Communist Party leader, Steve Nelson. The word lesbian wasn't mentioned until 3 August 1966 in an unfortunately titled review, *Sniggers for Sister George*. The article was actually a relatively positive commentary on the play *The Killing of Sister George*, set partly in the famous London lesbian club Gateways.

Starting in Depression, the 1930s ended in war. The 1940s started in war and ended with the use of troops against the Communist-led Miners' strike of 1949. While the CPA had some expectation that the post-WWII period could mirror the revolutionary times after WWI, governments and employers, fearing just such a revolution, stepped up their anti-Communist attack. The CPA was hammered for its role in the Miners' strike and soon found itself literally fighting for its life. The party had already been banned for a time during WWII and in 1951 faced yet another attempt, with more to come. The use of laws such as the Crimes Act saw leading members jailed, and the tight censorship which operated during the War wasn't really lifted till the late 1960s.

The end of the unknowing

However for homosexuals, Gary Wotherspoon suggests there was a change in a more positive direction. He sees two events during the 1940s as pivotal for the future. The first was WWII which provided many women and men with a wider range of sexual experiences, including for many homoerotic sexuality and love for the first time. The war, he says "acted as a catalyst for dramatic changes in social... and in particular sexual behaviour".[40] There was more space for cruising and while the police closed venues, new ones were soon open. In one case patrons fought the cops in a virtual riot.[41]

The second was the release in 1948 of the first Kinsey Report on male sexual behaviour, which demonstrated just how widespread homosexual experiences were in modern society. These two events Wotherspoon writes make the 1940s such an important decade in Australia's social history; "it marks the 'end to unknowing' about homoeroticism and homosexuality in Australia."[42] Whether the "knowing" had actually started in the 1920s is a moot point, but there's no doubt the forties pushed open the closet door. Internationally the post war period marked a revival of homosexual rights organising, especially in the US and UK, a revival which was to lay the basis for the modern Gay Liberation movement. However the situation in Australia at this time, while involving a certain freeing up, didn't duplicate the overseas experience of forming gay rights groups.

Into the 1950s, the CPA's political project found itself under severe pressure, not just from the Cold War, but from within its own ranks. News came from Russia and its satellite states of events which began to expose cracks in the Soviet edifice. First came Stalin's death in 1953 and new leader Krushchev's revelations in 1956 of Stalin's repressive and murderous regime. Then came the uprisings in Poland and more famously Hungary in 1956 and the subsequent repression by Russian tanks, leading to deep divisions within the CPA and mass resignations.

Far from being dull, as many describe or remember it, the 1950s proved to be just as a political and sexually challenging a decade as the archetypal "political"1960s.

Sexuality had never entirely gone off the agenda and was now flamboyantly displayed in mainstream society as Rock and Roll hit the airwaves. Rebellious young people – the so-called bodgies and widgies – were backed by the CPA when they were censured by the press. *Tribune* wrote that "attempts at individual expression as a form of personal revolt against capitalism are not peculiar to this generation". It contrasted the rebels of the 50s to the "lairs and larrikins" of the early 1900s who "came good" in the fight against conscription in 1916-1917; or the "jazz babies" of the 1920s who joined the struggles in the Depression, some becoming active socialists.

The paper argued that the rebellious behaviour of young people in the 1950s had a legitimate cause. "Facing our bodgie boys right now is the threat of being conscripted for up to five years under Menzies National Service Bill" to be sent to fight America's battles "anywhere in the world".[43]

But homosexuality was still a hidden topic. Literature with lesbian and gay content or by known homosexual writers, such as Han Suyin's *Winter Love*, Radclyffe Hall's *Adam's Breed*, Oscar Wilde's works, the poetry of Laurie Collinson and Walt Whitman continued to be listed by *Tribune* without once mentioning homosexuality. The paper ran a critical article about The Kinsey Report on Women, having completely ignored Kinsey's earlier examination of male sexuality. Not that they were alone in ignoring Kinsey's first book. One of the few Australian papers to cover it was the racy tabloid *Truth*, headlining its review, "Sex book is dynamite".[44]

Throughout the 1960s, as the Communist Party welcomed the global youth rebellion, the references to sex and, for the first time, drugs, increased in its publications and the Party started having meetings about these topics. However with only four explicit mentions of homosexuality in *Tribune*, and only one of them positive, the paper's approach of the 1950s continued, the oblique references recognised only by those "in the know".

In this they lagged the Church of England and debate on some of the campuses. At Melbourne University in 1964 the Student Debating Union considered the case for and against homosexual law reform and when the vote was taken it was 281 yes, with 98 no.[45]

But the party was on the brink of major change and Lance Gowland's story gives us a picture of being gay in the CPA at that time. Lance was based in the NSW town of Goulburn, involved in the trade unions and secretary of the Goulburn Trades and Labour Council. With parents in the CPA, he'd been in the Eureka Youth League and Communist Youth League before joining the party himself. In his early days in the EYL and CPA he didn't identify as gay, but by the late 60s realisation that he was homosexual brought big changes in his life, without relinquishing his politics. However for Gowland being gay meant there were still some political obstacles. "A lot of us felt we were disenfranchised," neglected or even excluded. Gowland remembers that he and others "started to say, hey, what about us? We were against the American invasion of Vietnam", we wanted to be part of "the great upwelling of the social movement struggle".

Though he got a gay rights group going in Goulburn, coming out was hard in 1969. "The police were on to us and they were parked outside when we had meetings and they were raiding our homes..." Frustrated by the lack of progress in Goulburn, he started looking elsewhere for a more favourable terrain. So he moved in 1970, "cos everything was happening in Sydney...I was very excited by it and I wanted to come and join in, take part in it."[46] And it was the Gay Liberation movement coming from the US, linking its struggle with those of the North Vietnamese, the Blacks and Women, which provided just the movement for him.[47]

Another Party member who argued Gay Liberation's cause within the CPA was Phil Carswell. He describes an exciting time, something of a shake-up of the party – with greens, gays and women's libbers, "a general melee of change". While most of the support came from CPA women who'd been impacted by Women's Liberation, Phil believes the majority in the party weren't actually homophobic, they were progressive and open to challenges. 'I think what they saw was the fundamental oppression and the fundamental issues at stake here and said sure we don't particularly want to do it, but if it's an issue for you, go off and do it."⁴⁸

But the last word for the moment lies with Denis Freney. In a first for Australia, *Tribune* published Freney's "Gay Liberation" on 26 May 1971, five months before Australia's first GL group met. Beginning his article with Oscar Wilde's famous declaration of homosexuality as the love that dares not speak its name, Freney could be confident that that Love had spoken out, had truly Come of Age in Australia's Left.⁴⁹

Chapter 2

Desire, Shame and Rebellion

So many had hopes for the fifties; by and large these were dashed. Later, looking back, people saw the fifties as all bad, but that wasn't true either. Historian and New York Lesbian Archives founder Joan Nestle got the balance right when she described the era before Gay Liberation as one of "desire, shame, rebellion, sometimes all at once". "History", she added, "never stays in its place, it's always moving, always waiting for us to pick it up."[1]

From the beginning to World War II

Our modern history started "publicly" in 1869 when the word homosexual was coined. Of course, such naming didn't create homosexuals. Many during the 1800s saw themselves as homosexual, using other descriptions such as intermediate sex, invert, third sex and "Urning", while the Molly Houses of 1700s London attest to an earlier self-identification. Homosexual behaviour has appeared in every society, but the labelling of a person as "a homosexual" was part of the development of social relations within capitalism. Homosexuality over time has been variously valued, incorporated within religious rituals or simply accepted. But homosexual acts have also been criminalised, demonised or regarded as sinful by the authorities, all with the view of eliminating such behaviour. Treatment as an illness came with the rise of scientific enquiry into the natural world, including human behaviour. Gay men have faced most of society's opprobrium, whereas until recently lesbianism has rarely been rarely spoken about by church or state. Despite the silence, however, lesbians have been castigated as sinful or subject to medical treatment. While not always directly criminalising lesbianism, the state has used "offences" such as "indecent assault", "obscene behaviour" and many a lesbian has been sacked from her job simply because she was gay.

Same-sex attracted people have not just stood by in the face of their treatment by church, state or medicine – the "sinner, criminal or sickness" framework. In England where the laws were particularly harsh, the Order of Chaerona was founded in 1897 as a secret club to act as a social group and to fight for "The Cause" (law reform). But it was not until 1958 that an open organisation of homosexuals campaigning for law reform appeared. Early colonial Australia inherited Britain's anti-sodomy laws with their long jail terms and death penalty, but there was no reform group until the late 1960s, 180 years after colonisation.[2]

Before World War Two, the world's biggest reform movement was in Germany. Homosexuals and supporters founded the Scientific and Humanitarian Committee in 1897 to fight newly introduced anti-homosexual laws, and Magnus Hirschfeld's Institute of Sex Research was set up in 1919. Both the Committee and the Institute were actively supported by the German Social Democratic Party and both fell foul of the Nazis.[3] Before suffering this fate, the German movement inspired Henry Gerber, a recent migrant to the US to found the Society for Human Rights in 1924 in Chicago. The group put out two issues of its magazine *Friendship and Freedom* but was then "uncovered", broken up and Gerber and some of its members prosecuted. Though eventually acquitted, Gerber lost his job and all his money in the process, but did not give up the fight. During the early thirties he wrote for German magazines, in the 1940s translated some of Hirschfeld's book and even produced a couple of pamphlets arguing for gay rights. He never tried to set up another organisation. As soon as the Mattachine Society was set up in 1950 he joined, though he never took a leading role again.[4]

White picket fences or "the most political time of my life"

Many, on both the left and right, believed the aftermath of the Second World War would resemble that of WWI – revolution and economic crisis. The revolution in China and resurgent Communist Parties in Europe gave hope to millions around the globe. But instead there was post-war occupation, war and the threat of annihilation by atomic weapons. A Cold War developed, a facing off of the two major post-war powers, Russia (USSR) and America, with proxy wars such as Korea and Vietnam. Repressive measures targeted the left and other dissidents, with thousands sacked from their jobs and many jailed, while the heterosexual nuclear family was heavily reinforced. Vice – homosexuality, drugs, pornography and prostitution – rather than exploitation and war was presented as the real threat in the post-war era. The Oxford Dictionary of 1951, for example, listed Sunday shopping and entertainment along with prostitution, drugs and homosexuality as threats to the social fabric.[5]

In retrospect the 1950s are often portrayed as embodying all that is conservative, complacent and conventional. Marilyn Lake writes about Australia that "The decade of the 1950s has come to be equated with the uninterrupted rule of the prime minister, R G Menzies, the waging of the Cold War at home and abroad and the 'traditional' role of women – who, as submissive wives and conscientious mothers, exclaimed over their new electrical appliances and cleaning aids, happy in their condition of house arrest..."[6]

But as we know from Betty Friedan's *The Feminine Mystique* and Simone de Beauvoir's *The Second Sex* and from campaigns such as the anti-nuclear movement and the battles against attempts to ban the Communist Party, there is another side to this period. Lake continues:

"Yet in attributing such uniformity and homogeneity to a decade, in accusing it of such self-satisfied complacency, the conventional view fails to acknowledge the social and political insurrections that provoked the very repressions the critics denounce... Those who would characterise the 1950s as a dreary, dull and dutiful decade miss its vital significance for gender relations."⁷

It was a time when women were increasingly drawn into the workforce. The novel *Bobbin Up* by CPA member Dorothy Hewett about factory life illustrates the self-assertiveness and rebelliousness amongst some of these 1950s women workers.

Unlike earlier eras where only men's sexual lives were recognised, in post-WWII society, both women and men were encouraged – albeit only within marriage – to have fulfilling sex lives. It was also considered a very modern time, with many scientific and technological developments changing the way people lived their lives. In *Imagining the Fifties* John Murphy says that "Ideas of what was modern played a key part in this model of marriage as partnership. Many of the arguments women journalists made in defence of equal pay, of married women's right to work and of the idea of equality within marriage were framed as rights, resistance to which was outdated and pre-modern. Thus they spoke of only a 'die-hard' disputing women's right to work and condemned those men 'clinging to the old idea of wifely possession'."⁸

But at the same time marriage and women's role in the home were promoted. The 1950s family was also a step back, Murphy notes: "The image of marriage as a private, self-contained partnership, as an intimate commonwealth of two, was a marked contraction from the solidarities and public identities of the war and the post-war reconstruction period...." This process was part of breaking down working class collectivity and encouraging the notion of "the individual" within society. It was a way of heading off class antagonism and working class solidarity that had developed during the 1930s and 1940s.⁹

The conventional view of the fifties as unchanging and conformist additionally fails to grasp that the post-war 1940s through to the early 1950s, were unstable with an ever present threat of economic crisis, job insecurity, wages pressure and attacks on unionisation. Until the mid-50s, promises of post-war prosperity were largely uncertain promises. "Growth and full employment were marred by inflation and shortages and by doubts that a depression might return", writes Murphy. "This period of anxiety coincided with the most turbulent and fearful period of the Cold War...when – across the political spectrum – many feared another world war." The fabled post-war boom came afterwards. [10]

Attacks on the CPA, popular ally of Australia's rulers for much of WWII, began soon after. Under the post-war Chifley ALP government, the party was ferociously condemned for its role in the 1949 coal miners' strike. The next year the new conservative Prime Minister Robert Menzies tried to ban the Communists, creating a climate where the party was demonised, with raids on its premises and homes of leading members. Censorship was stepped up and left wing texts deemed seditious and prohibited. Known and suspected CPA members were sacked or refused employment and sometimes jailed.

But it made for a very politicised time and some union battles won important gains. At a few workplaces there was a serious fight to retain women's higher war-time rates of pay and apart from a short period when women were shed from the workforce, their employment rate continued to rise. One woman on a radio program celebrating 50 years of ABC television recalled this as one of the most political and exciting times of her life.

Many of those wanting to fight back against injustice looked to the Communist Party. Even when attitudes towards women were sometimes "awful", as Dorothy Hewett recalled, she acknowledged that "the sort of women attracted into the Communist Party were strong, passionate and revolutionary...it was possible within the Party for women to act with a lot more force than in any other political area."[11] Phyllis Johnson's participation in the Party gave her a "knowledge that few women possess".

"They [women outside the CPA] know nothing about the tactics of political movements, of being able to assess and analyse a question, to take it a little further in its development, to see what the objectives are and how to go about achieving a tactical objective. I learnt all this in the CPA."[12]

Students also took to the streets. There was a huge demonstration on the eve of the 1956 Melbourne Olympics. Their banners condemned British PM, Anthony Eden for sending troops into Suez, Russia's Krushchev for rolling the tanks into Budapest and the threats from Russia to bomb London.[13]

For homosexuals the 1950s were both symbols of repression and yet also of a certain freedom – and even the promise of something better.

The war had opened up a whole new social scene, a "social revolution in the gay and lesbian subculture," writes Clive Moore. Instead of the more closeted private gatherings, hotels and other public places became the places to meet others and despite the repression of the Cold War period "the gay subculture continued to strengthen".[14] But while the social scene grew after the war, there was still no attempt to build a political or law reform group in Australia, unlike the US and UK.

American gays protest

The aftermath of war in America marked the beginnings of openly gay political organisation. Although the witchhunts were severe, lasting several decades until the 1970s, the 1950s saw homosexuals form their own gay rights group, the Mattachine Society. Founded in 1950 by Harry Hay, a couple of fellow CPUSA members and other activists, they brought to the group some of the ideas and practices of the Communist Party. These early activists saw homosexuals as a "class" or social group, asserting that unless gays began to view themselves as proud members of a group, rather than as sinners, criminals or deviants, they would not want to be part of a gay rights movement. Hay described the first meeting on 11 November, 1950: "We sat there, with fire in our eyes and far-away dreams, *being* Gays".[15]

From the heritage of the left, they understood that social change came through mass action, hence the need to build a movement, "a large gay constituency that was capable of militancy." The purpose of the society, outlined in their one-page document of April 1951, was "to unify isolated homosexuals, educate homosexuals to see themselves as an oppressed minority and lead them in a struggle for their own emancipation".[16]

Mattachine in its earlier years, though not taking to the streets like the later protests, was involved in some important challenges to homosexual discrimination.[17] In 1952 the Society ran its first public "protest". Founding member Dale Jennings had been arrested on a beat. He refused to plead guilty, instead accusing the police of entrapment. Mattachine members handed out fliers at venues around town, as well as placing money jars prominently in gay bars to help fund a legal defence. These fliers were, according to Belinda Baldwin, probably "the first to politicise an individual's arrest as a gay rights issue". The case went to trial, Jennings admitted he was homosexual but pleaded not guilty to the charge. The jury was deadlocked, Jennings got off and Mattachine claimed its first victory.[18]

Jennings explored the larger implications of his trial in the first issue of *ONE* magazine:

"Were all homosexuals and bisexuals to unite militantly, unjust laws and corruption would crumble in short order...Were heterosexuals to realize that these violations of our rights threaten theirs equally, a vast reform might even come within our lifetime. This is no more a dream than trying to win a case after admitting homosexuality."[19]

The Daughters of Bilitis, the first lesbian group, began in 1955, initially as a social club and then as a political grouping, though more low key than Mattachine or One Inc (a breakaway from Mattachine). In an attempt to push DOB into a more activist stance one member, a Karla Marx, wrote a Lesbian Manifesto – based on the Communist Manifesto – a daring act in Cold War America.[20] Both Mattachine and DOB were to be involved in much more public events from the 1960s, but during the 1950s they mostly published magazines, ran social events and provided support for those victimised by the state and employers. And they grew, reaching memberships in the thousands.

The decade ended in America with the first known gay riot.

In May 1959, police moved in one night to Coopers Donuts, an all-night hangout in downtown Los Angeles, frequented by young hustlers and drag queens. Author John Rechy described how these hustlers and drag queens resisted, throwing food and tableware and forcing the cops to retreat to their cars. The police had to call for reinforcements and close the street before they could make their arrests.[21]

Australia - the paradox of repression

In the UK it wasn't until 1958, in the wake of the Wolfenden Enquiry (see below), that two homosexual groups were formed: the Albany Trust (a counselling group also open to non-homosexuals) and the Homosexual Law Reform Society.

Australian homosexuals established no reform groups, but there were flow-on effects from international events that brought about significant change. The1940s had half opened the closet door, with WWII and the Kinsey Report alerting many lesbians and homosexuals that they weren't alone in the world. Gary Wotherspoon describes these events as bringing an "end of the unknowing". They were followed in the 1950s by two developments – the increased repression of the Cold War – which paradoxically forced a further opening of the closet door - and the Wolfenden enquiry.

The increased repression, including the efforts to stamp out homosexuality during the Cold War, Wotherspoon argues, "had exactly the opposite effect in the long run. The heightened profile for all things homosexual that all this activity created eventually led to greater public discourse, leading in turn to changed ideas within our society as to what homosexuality represented."[22]

While the main target of the Cold War was the working class and its organisations, including the Communist Party, conservative forces also waged a propaganda war on two fronts – the supposed threat from outside and the threat from within, a threat to the nation's moral fibre.

In 1951, privately backed by Menzies, a group of chief justices and church leaders issued a "Call to Australia". Printed in every newspaper with editorial support and broadcast across the nation on the eve of Remembrance Day, the "Call" told Australians they were in danger. "We are in danger from abroad. We are in danger at home. We are in danger from moral and intellectual apathy, from the mortal enemies of mankind... [which] demand a restoration of the moral order from which alone the social order can derive."[23]

To counter the threat from outside, Menzies oversaw rearmament, development of national industries for self-sufficiency, national service for all 18-year old men and continued armed intervention in countries to the north. To counter the threat from within, apart from directly targeting the left and unions, the government ramped up censorship, surveillance and police campaigns against vice.

They had willing partners in the police. In almost every state, police chiefs pronounced on the dire moral decline facing society – from Adelaide's claim to be the "sex crime city" to NSW's Chief Commissioner Colin Delaney's 1958 statement that homosexuality was the "greatest menace". The police were ably abetted by the press, with high profile stories of the arrests.[24]

NSW led the pack. Commissioner Delaney had a long history of policing vice. With close ties to the UK and probable employment in wartime Intelligence Services, Delaney took over control of the NSW police force at a time when it was under intense scrutiny, accused of bribery, corruption and violence.[25]

Delaney was an empire builder, always calling for extra funding and greater police powers, using supposed threats to society to bolster his case. As a Chief Superintendant in 1951 he'd flagged the "alarming" increase of male homosexuals and by 1952 he claimed male homosexuality was a threat to Australian society, equal only to that of Communism. Nothing was more guaranteed to improve police statistics than arresting gay men, as the crime was "solved" immediately on charging, with no need for lengthy investigations. Arrest numbers could be increased at will simply by increasing the numbers of police targeting known homosexual beats. In December 1953 Delaney ordered all 84 members of Sydney's Vice Squad to almost full-time duty of locating the "haunts of homosexuals".

By 1957 there were 688 convictions in NSW, almost two a day.²⁶

Naomi Cranenburgh's thesis *From Invisible to 'Menace':Lesbians in Australia from 1939 to 1965*, also points out that during this time lesbians were targeted for policing and persecution. "This increased vigour in policing meant that the veil of official silence was lifted: Female homosexuals (as with their brothers) were subject to marked surveillance, as well as many other measures of abuse and violation. This demonisation marked a turning point in Australian lesbian history..."²⁷

Male homosexuals were subject to specific anti-homosexual offences. Policing of lesbians, except for a few notable cases in the armed forces, was individual, "discreet" and used more general charges such as offensive behaviour. This meant there was no basis for a law reform movement amongst lesbians, though the greater number of charges did encourage a certain politicisation. Most tried to live "under the radar", although their lives were becoming more public and "risky" as they frequented the cafes of St Kilda and the city. Those that were politically minded, though not about their sexuality, joined other causes and organisations, including the Communist Party.²⁸

Some church figures, lawyers and civil libertarians were expressing growing disquiet about the so-called "victimless crimes" of prostitution, homosexuality and abortion (divorce and suicide were often included), both in Australia and the UK. Apart from condemning the rampant corruption around policing prostitution and abortion, there was increasing debate about what role the state should have in individual's lives. In Australia a national law conference in 1952 stated that sex between consenting adult males did not pose a threat to society. And in 1956, a Church of England report declared that there was "no evidence that homosexual practices are more harmful than normal sex practices".²⁹

Contradictions of the fifties

In England these issues came to a head in 1953, after a spike in prosecutions and a scandal associated with the arrest of several prominent gay men in London over sexual liaisons with airforce personnel and young working class men. Another of the victimless crimes was also in the headlines, with ruling class concern over increased street soliciting by prostitutes caused by post-war economic hardships.

The Tory government set up a Committee, headed by Lord Wolfenden, to investigate homosexuality and prostitution. Its findings were brought down on 4 September 1957. The recommendations included a reduction in many of the penalties and decriminalisation of sex between men over 21, in private. But it proposed increasing the penalties for female street prostitutes and criminalising male prostitution.

The recommendations for homosexuals weren't acceptable to the Tory government (despite the committee being stacked with conservatives). More welcome were the increased penalties for street prostitution (female and male) and the government passed them into law in 1959. It was to take till 1967, under Harold Wilson's Labour government, for Wolfenden's recommendations on homosexuality to be made law. However, the changes were criticised by some in the increasingly visible gay community. Gay historian Jeffrey Weeks describes it as an attempt to strengthen state control of morality at a time when the Church of England and some other Protestant churches were claiming it for themselves. The Archbishop of Canterbury, Dr. Fisher, declared that "There is a sacred realm of privacy...into which the law, generally speaking, must not intrude. This is a principle of the utmost importance for the preservation of human freedom, self-respect, and responsibility."[30]

Limitations aside – the higher age of consent, the fact that the law was only applicable in England and Wales and the exclusion of the armed services – the worst thing about the new law was that the number of gay men arrested actually increased. Under the narrow provision of "in private" in the new law, sex in public places (bars, beats, etc) was made a clear breach of the law, making it easier to arrest and sentence homosexuals.

On the positive side, Wolfenden prompted the formation in 1958 of the Homosexual Law Reform Society (HLRS), the first public political group of homosexuals in Britain. And as we'll see, the first attempts in Australia that we know of, to set up a similar group.

The British scandals, the establishment of the Wolfenden Committee and the later 1967 legalisation were covered in Australia and not just in the tabloid press. A sympathetic review of the Committee's Report in *People* magazine, claimed the world would be a worse place without well-known homosexuals in society. While *People* also talked about a "violent controversy" both in Australia and England, it also pointed to the unwelcome fact that the English-speaking nations were notable for their condemnation and criminalisation of homosexuality.[31]

There was support for law reform amongst some in Australian society. Was this matched by a similar response from the CPA? In short the answer is no. While the party's opposition to censorship and its more progressive stance more generally in relation to women and Indigenous Australians would normally have put it on the side of homosexual emancipation, the impact of Stalinism meant that its Stalinist pro-family position tended to align it with more conservative calls to "defend" the family.

Its response to the Kinsey Report illustrates this contradiction. When Alfred Kinsey first released his studies on male sexuality in 1948, *Tribune* was silent, but it gave nearly full page coverage to his second on female sexuality in 1953. Critical of Kinsey, it wrote "Their appetites whetted by his earlier book on 'Sexual Behaviour in the Human Male', the capitalist press seized hungrily on his similar study of the Human female... His subject was Sex – the staple food in capitalist cultural diet." The article questioned his statistics and claimed his result had no relationship to genuine science, adding that "they don't take us one step nearer to social morality or stable sexual relations".

"Kinsey presents his subjects in a vacuum – but they don't live in a vacuum, they live in the US," *Tribune* wrote. "They are women who face a day of grinding toil and nagging worry as to how they are to feed and clothe their children and themselves. They are reminded constantly by every available means that their sex is a marketable commodity. All of the women, and their men, are subject to the 'psychological war' of the Wall Street war planners."

There is certainly some truth in *Tribune*'s commentary, but they saw nothing positive in Kinsey's research. The reviewer didn't see that for lesbians (and gay men and his first book), knowing that there were others like them was so important. Instead they turned to Russia for a glowing comparison of women's situation there. *Tribune* asserted, children were cared for, mothers were valued, women workers had equal pay and conditions. The paper cited Engels as offering more in a few pages as a way for the future than the two volumes of Kinsey. But the party had to explain away tighter divorce laws and re-criminalisation of abortion in Russia, unlike what they campaigned for in Australia. It argued that motherhood was feted in many ways, including the issuing of medals such as "Order of Mother's Glory" and "Heroine Mother", all of which signified that women and men were treated as equals. Consequently, the party argued, it meant that in Russia there was no longer the need for divorce or abortion.[32]

The party publicly expressed a somewhat puritanical attitude to sex, but it defended young people against the moral panic and hysterical attacks in the press. The *Sunday Sun* was roundly condemned for attacking widgies (rebellious young working class women) and their dress style on the back cover, while running an advertisement inside promoting just such clothes for teenage girls. "Typical of our hypocritical press", *Tribune* wrote. "Publicise erotic behaviour, play up sex and then with righteous indignation condemn the morals of the day that they helped to corrupt." [33]

The party's Eureka Youth League argued that Cold War propaganda was partly to blame for so-called juvenile delinquency because it encouraged an attitude of "live for today, for tomorrow we may be blasted to bits". They also attacked comics, magazines, film and radio serials for "glorifying sadism and sex and for fostering hatred of other peoples". Again there's some truth in this commentary, but it lacked an understanding of the underlying sexual rebellion. It was a mixture of progressive thought on the impact of war and racism, with a more "prudish" attitude to sex from the EYL that ended up repelling many young people they'd won over through their anti-war stance.[34]

Tribune carried ten articles during the 1950s that could be said to generally refer to homosexuality, including the Kinsey Report. Of the ten, two articles mentioning homosexuality itself referred either to someone who was a scab or to the book-burning (Chapter Two). A third was ambiguous, a mention of the hated Joe McCarthy, the instigator of witchhunts against communists in the US. A further two attacked Stephen Spender, who, at least until 1941 was known to be gay and had been close the British Communist Party. However Spender was attacked, not for homosexuality (nor was it mentioned), but because he was accused of abandoning communism. The other three mentions, none of which referred to homosexuality, included two reviews of Laurie Collinson's poems and a review of Walt Whitman; a novel with lesbian references by Han Suyin and *Adam's Breed* by lesbian writer Radclyffe Hall were listed in Tribune's "books for sale".

A number of other reviews touched on sex and sexuality in films, books or shows by visiting pop stars. *Tribune* book listings regularly included classics such as *The Decameron* or *1001 Nights*, Oscar Wilde or Moll Flanders, as well as more modern novels. There were reviews of films such as *The Blue Angel* with Marlene Dietrich, *Jailhouse Rock* and *A Streetcar Named Desire*. To counter these were the stories of more "wholesome" Soviet and Eastern Bloc life, marriage manuals and the like, an attempt at a communist morality. One such marriage manual was the popular guidebook by British doctors, Abraham and Hannah Stone. While their manual did describe homosexuality as a "congenital abnormality", they explicitly countered the stereotypes: "The majority of homosexual men and women have the appearance, characteristics, and physique of their own sex..." This was not mentioned by *Tribune*.[35]

In *Pinks under the Bed, a study of homosexuality, communism and the nation state during the Cold War in Australia*, Kate Davison argues: "Communists in Australia were acting...within the conservative framework built up during the Stalin era," adding that "In relation to homosexuality, one of the ways these policies manifested in the CPA was, ironically, in the striking duplication of the policies and strategies of the Australian state."[36] While this is partly correct, it is clear the CPA opposed many of the state's strategies, including censorship. The examples above of the CPA's coverage in *Tribune* show a more contradictory picture. It legitimately criticised the hypocrisy of the government over censorship and its targeting of left wing literature and film. As well it was correct to situate its critique of the Kinsey Report with commentary on women's oppression under capitalism, noting how women's lives left little time for the joys of sexual relationships. Where the Party failed was in its uncritical acceptance, even glorification, of the views of the family by the Stalinist regimes. This led it – in the absence of a mass movement campaigning for gay rights – into its more negative view of homosexuality from the 1930s to the mid 1960s. That is when they addressed it at all.

Gay inside the CPA

The actual experience of homosexuals within the CPA during the 1950s and 1960s is also contradictory. Davison gives examples of people who were discovered as homosexuals by the Party and then dropped or given the "silent treatment". Others, however, were never asked to leave, as with Rod Anderson, keeping their homosexuality hidden when they joined. Some homosexual members while critical of the CPA's attitudes, did not leave. Colin, as quoted by Davison, claimed the Party was "just as homophobic as the intelligence organisations that were supposedly monitoring them", but he stayed a member. The Cold War scandals of Burgess and Maclean, British spies who defected to Russia and were later exposed as homosexuals, along with the general paranoia of the day, seemed to confirm – and partially justify – the Party's opposition to homosexuality according to another member Brian. And Rae recalls worrying about how the sexual orientation of Soviet spies "was going to affect the homosexual cause, just when we were trying to get through that we were 'decent, honest' people who just wanted to 'live our lives'."[37]

Certainly Party members were aware of the security risks. When Judah Waten recalled that "there was no shortage of gays", another reminded him "there was a bit of a worry about them...because being gay was not accepted and they were subject to police lifts". But attitudes varied widely within the CPA, from calling them "artistic freaks" or "those poofters" as Bob Besant did, to acceptance. Edna Ryan recalled "trying to find the right line from [Party leader] Higgins". She asked, "The Russians don't mind about men being homosexual, do they?" only to get the response "Oh well, I don't really know".[38]

In *Free Radical*, Rod describes how he joined the Party after the war. He wanted socialism but had doubts about personal freedom under communism. After some discussion and CP-run classes, he was convinced about "the need to overthrow capitalism with a revolutionary party". "But the Party," he adds, "regarded homosexuals as immoral and degenerate. If I joined, I would have to conceal my interest in other men and behave as though I was completely square. This was a concession I was prepared to make. I joined the Communist Party of Australia."

On the other hand, when he joined the campus section of the Party after becoming a student as part of the returned soldiers' scheme, he found many in the branch regarded promiscuous sex as a revolutionary act.[39]

The paradox for the Party was that there were members everyone knew were gay. Both Edna Ryan and Barbara Curthoys recall such members who were accepted locally, but the issue was "shrouded in silence" as Damousi describes. The Party did not "further their campaigns", but Edna Ryan believed "we had no view, there was no lobby about homosexuals". Both Ryan and Curthoys insist that homosexual members were not condemned as people and few supported any "snide comments" that were made; nor would the Party have joined in persecution of lesbians or homosexual men.⁴⁰

Nonetheless the CPA did expel members and refuse to renew membership of homosexuals. It is not the case though, as the previous examples indicate, that this was "indicative of its overall approach to homosexuality" as Kate Davison argues. More likely, those thought to be security risks in a party itself "at risk" of repressive reaction from the State, were the ones pushed out, while others in associated groups such as the New Theatre were left alone. One prominent case which did result in expulsion was when Charles Bresland, national secretary of the Party's youth wing – the Eureka Youth League – was arrested after being found passed out in a Sydney toilet. He was "persuaded" by the police to plead guilty and was then convicted of indecent behaviour. Bresland lost his position in the EYL and despite trying to win a position on the Central Committee later in 1958 was expelled from the Party, never to be a member again. There was no explanation from the party leadership when Bresland went. But one member recalls the leadership rarely commented when members went underground or were expelled for "deviations" from the Party line, there were just "sudden silences". There is an ambiguous reference in the Central Committee minutes to "that other filthy charge of offensive behaviour" which could be read either as condemnation of Bresland, or condemnation of the charge. It is not clear whether what happened within the Party was the result of homophobia or a measure to protect the Party during the Cold War era. Bresland had already been under surveillance by Special Branch and ASIO, though there is no reference in their reports to his being homosexual. At any rate this was not the right thing for the party to do.⁴¹

We may never know the exact circumstances surrounding Bresland's case. But for Rod Anderson, in the CPA from 1945-1962, the risks to the party partially justified its attitude. Because the party was "under attack so much, they had to be careful – that's got a lot to do with the Party's 'slightly puritanical' attitude to sex". As to whether the party should have supported law reform, he felt gays hadn't joined the CPA to change these laws. Rather, while change would come, it was still some decades in the future and so it wasn't necessary to put gay rights demands on the agenda right then and there. He also considered it less a "political" issue than a "social" one and felt that for the party it was the same.

Teacher and CP sympathiser Bill Leslie argues that there were real limits to what organising at that time could have achieved. He comments that you could only speak about homosexuality "in the context of crime". You couldn't do more, he adds. Also you couldn't organise amongst gays until "homosexuals became self-aware". You needed that before you could talk about homosexuality in a different context.[42]

Nonetheless Anderson believes there was the possibility of a Wolfenden-style enquiry developing in Australia, adding "If I'd been active around homosexual law reform while I was in the party, at the time I probably thought I would have been asked to leave...But looking back on it I doubt that I would."

Wolfenden did inspire another homosexual CPA member, Laurie Collinson, to attempt to found a law reform group in Australia. Collinson whose poems had been favourably reviewed in *Tribune*, had been an activist and poet from his school days, joining the CPA first in Brisbane and then rejoining in Melbourne in the forties. In 1958 he wrote to the UK HLRS asking for assistance and gathered the names of a number of gay and non-gay supporters in Australia. None, however, were prepared to go public and the project collapsed before it could get off the ground.[43]

Anderson, Collinson's partner at the time, supported his activities around law reform. He says, "The Communist Party would have had to be blind not to know about Laurie's involvement in law reform, but they would have just said, 'it's not our concern, we're in politics, not sex'."

Overall, says Anderson, "I think a lot went on that wasn't spoken about". While he was never asked to leave the Party for his homosexuality, it appears Collinson was refused membership when he went to renew it, possibly because of his sexual orientation, or his activities around law reform. Collinson left for London in 1964, never to return. Anderson left in 1962 from a country he felt was "so conservative, conformist, dull", only returning in the late 1970s to a very changed Australia.[44]

It seems Collinson kept his more radical beliefs alive and when Gay Liberation hit London some years later, he was full of praise. Contrasting it to the more reformist Campaign for Homosexual Equality, he said. "CHE is an organisation; GLF is a way of life".[45]

CHAPTER 3

GENERATION ON FIRE. THE SIXTIES

Quintessentially the time of revolt, the sixties certainly didn't start with a bang. If the early 1950s had been unsettled and volatile, by the late 1950s the economy had moved into boom and society was, at least on the surface, more staid and conservative. Anti-union laws were taking a toll, industrial action was ebbing, jobs, wages and conditions were stabilising, even increasing. And this flowed into the 1960s. If anything the boom seemed more entrenched and strike figures continued to drop. A heavy blanket of conservatism seemed to smother all cultural expression, with censorship in full swing. In Europe Andre Gorz, a leading French Marxist intellectual, wrote off hope of revolutionary change: "It is unlikely that in the foreseeable future there will be a crisis in capitalism so acute that, in order to protect their vital interests, workers will resort to a revolutionary general strike or armed insurrection."[1]

Yet only two years after Gorz's pronouncement France was to explode in a huge student protest and general strike. It was followed by the Czechoslovak uprising and then world-wide protests, peaking with the Portuguese Revolution of 1974. Earlier than this, as Betty Friedan and Simone de Beauvoir's books had indicated, there were clear signs that discontent was growing, that dissatisfaction with the home in the suburbs lifestyle was rife.

In Australia the winds of change came with the students and young workers. Post-war, the population had surged; a quarter of the population was under 25, the most it had – and has – ever been. And from that there was a massive influx into education, university student numbers rising from 12,000 to 30,000 with another 35,000 in apprenticeships and teacher training. New universities out in the suburbs drew in young people from families who previously had only ever dreamt of going to university.

As the numbers on the campuses rose, so did the level of political engagement. At Melbourne University in July 1962, the *Farrago* editor Patrick McCaughey was "gaoled" in a cage by apolitical engineering students, incensed that he was publishing political material in the student newspaper, instead of the more usual trivia.[2]

On the job, young workers met experienced CP and ALP left members, rank and file activists and shop stewards who were to play a vital role in the upsurge of the late 1960s. On the campuses, the organised left were also there, the CPA vying for influence against the Maoist-aligned group and by the late 1960s against the newly emerging Trotskyist current. All appealing to young minds wanting new experiences, new ideas.

Communists

Whether it was the target of repression or a mobilising centre, the Communist Party was the strongest left wing political force in Australia for most of its existence (1920 to 1991). However the party's influence had begun to wane, with membership dropping to 12000 from the late 1940s and half that number by 1956. It was in decline from 1985 to its end in 1991.[3]

While the Russian invasion of Hungary in 1956 shook the CPA, it didn't split until 1963, when a pro-Beijing group broke away to form the CPA-ML (or Maoists). A second split followed the Soviet Union's use of tanks to crush the "Prague Spring" in 1968. This second split, in 1971, gave rise to the pro-Moscow Socialist Party of Australia. There were now three Communist parties. Of these, the CPA was the most supportive of and involved in the new liberation movements such as Women's Liberation. Neither the CPA(ML) nor the SPA supported the Gay Liberation movement, with the CPA(ML) actively hostile on some university campuses.[4]

The CPA was also facing external challengers. New Trotskyist groups were forming. The first was the youth group Resistance in 1967. Influenced by the US-based Socialist Workers Party, Resistance was the forerunner of the Australian Socialist Workers Party. By the early 1970s a second group appeared, the International Socialists which was closer to the British Trotskyist SWP.[5]

As Tom O'Lincoln outlines in his history of the party, "Wherever you looked the CPA was being outflanked and as the party leadership began to grasp the fact, it realised it faced something of a crisis. Its cadres had survived the Cold War partly by sticking to the hope of an eventual new left upsurge; it had also begun to liberalise and break with Moscow and naturally expected this to pay off in recruitment among the newly radicalising forces. Now it appeared the party would miss the boat."[6]

The CPA's national leaders decided in 1968 that if the party was to have a future, it would have to enter the "hurly-burly of the left". They staged the Left Action Conference in 1969 which brought in some 700 people. Its initial stand on the Vietnam War however, had become a barrier to recruitment. Less militant than others, even in the ALP, the party's call to "stop the bombing, negotiate", fell far short of the main left-wing demand of immediate troop withdrawal. If it was to be relevant it had to drop this approach and take up more radical demands.

This shift helped re-legitimise the party amongst radical youth, though it didn't bring in as many new members as they'd hoped. But, important to the struggle for gay rights, the changing politics within the CPA attracted some of those grouped around then Trotskyist Denis Freney. At the party's Easter 1970 conference, Freney told delegates the meeting was historic, "marking the qualitative break of the CPA with Stalinism". He joined soon afterwards and began working on *Tribune.*[7]

If any one issue can be said to have dominated Australian political activity, it was Vietnam. Intertwined with opposition to the troop presence was anger over conscription. Young men of 18 could end up in the army, even in Vietnam, just because their birth date was chosen in a lottery. Women associated with the CPA formed Save Our Sons in 1965. From these beginnings a mass movement grew with hundreds of thousands on the streets and a radicalised layer of young workers and students.

The Aboriginal and Torres Strait Islander population was also increasing and many of the youth were moving to the cities where they provided the spark for actions such as the 1965 Freedom Rides. The CPA, especially its union members, was important in building support for the Aboriginal cause.[8]

Then came Women's Liberation. And always in the background was the flexing of working class power. The 1969 general strike protesting the jailing of Tramways' union leader Clarrie O'Shea, galvanised workers around the country. Worker militancy peaked in 1974 with the highest strike rate since 1919. The Party, through its influence in the unions played a pivotal role in this strike and building working class militancy more generally.[9]

As part of the CPA's attempts to get into the "hurly burly of the left" and to relate to the young people they were meeting on the jobs and campuses, it was changing its public face. The references to student issues, sex and drugs increased in its publications and the party started having meetings about these topics. In 1969, when Trotskyist Bob Gould was prosecuted for displaying drawings of Aubrey Beardsley and some of Michelangelo's in his shop, *Tribune* dared the censors by including some on its own pages. Denis Freney commented that "It was the first time that nudes...had appeared in *Tribune* – or any Communist Party paper elsewhere to my knowledge". Given the continuing debate within the CPA over its direction, Freney acknowledged that publishing the drawings would cause agitation amongst "the morality police" – in the party.[10]

Novelist and party member Frank Hardy joined the push for greater openness. In a letter to *Tribune* he quoted Engels' commentary on the German working class poet Georg Weerth. "In one thing Weerth was a master...expressing natural robust sensuousness and the joys of the flesh." Engels added "there will come a time when the German Socialists too will triumphantly get rid of the last trace of philistine prejudices and hypocritical moral prudery...[which] only serve as a cover for surreptitious obscenity...It is high time that at least the German workers get accustomed to speaking in a free and easy manner about the things they themselves do every day or night. They are natural, inevitable and highly pleasant things..." In Germany, Engels declared, people should talk about sexual matters "as frankly as the Romance people do, as Homer did, and Plato, Horace and Juvenal, the Old Testament and the *Neue Rheinische Zeitung*".[11]

On homosexuality *Tribune*'s earlier approach continued, with its oblique references recognised only by those "in the know", though it stopped short of condemnation. The number of articles in the sixties that related to homosexuality was half that of the previous decade. But other articles about "sex" questions rose, particularly in relation to women; by the end of the decade there were articles on the Women's Liberation movement. There was a long debate in *Tribune* about New Theatre's performance of "The Ballad of Angel's Alley", a somewhat bawdy play set in a brothel. *Tribune* also opposed the obscenity charges against *Oz* magazine in London, arguing it was about political censorship, not sex.[12]

Where homosexuality was mentioned, it was more positive. One article defended a young working class man, while criticising the police who'd entrapped him. Another condemned the use of slurs such as "you're a dunce and a poofter" during the training of conscripts. In 1966, the paper printed a relatively sympathetic review of the lesbian play "Sister George". The article was critical of the lack of a "searching analysis" of the "problem of lesbianism", but said the play approached the issue "in a rather sniggering and weak-wristed way itself". This was also a first for the use of the word lesbian on its pages.[13]

In its coverage of homosexuality the Party still lagged behind liberal society. It abstained from church and civil liberties groups' calls for law reform and CPA members do not appear to have been involved in the early debates that took part on some of the campuses.[14]

For Australian gays, the last half of the sixties condensed into a few short years the growth in awareness and political organising that had occurred in the US and UK over the previous twenty years. The decade ended in Australia, not just on the high note of a general strike and rise in working class combativeness, but with a first for homosexuals who "came out" ready to take a stand.

Breaking Out

The first political steps were more tentative than confrontational and most of the voices for change were heterosexual (or apparently so). There were increasing numbers of articles in the press arguing for homosexual law reform, one of the most notable directly taking on Police Chief Delaney's assertion of homosexuality as Australia's greatest menace. In 1965 journalist Gordon Hawkins asked why Australia hadn't joined the legal liberalisation that had occurred elsewhere. One by one he countered myths about homosexuality and refuted police claims. He questioned the repression against a group of people whose "principal distinguishing feature is simply that they prefer their own to the opposite sex". Even though he'd just detailed the state's role in maintaining society's anti-homosexual measures, Hawkins was pessimistic about the chances of change. Instead he saw men's "personal insecurity" about masculinity as causing hostility to homosexuals and leading to a lack of support for law reform. Nonetheless the journalist was voicing an increasing call for change. Among the NSW judiciary there was such disquiet about increasing court appearances that they convened a meeting of the legal profession, government and police. Calling for a halt to arrests for what the judges considered a minor offence, they proposed medical treatment be considered, rather than filling the country's courts and jails.[15]

The Rationalist and Humanist Societies pressed for legal reform of "victimless" crimes including abortion and homosexuality. In the first issue of *The Humanist* in December 1966, Beatrice Faust's article "Ethics vs Morality" argued that if there was a threat to society it came not from homosexuality, but from the laws against homosexuality. The law was "damaging to the social order it claimed to protect", impossible to administer fairly and encouraged corruption. This was not an endorsement of "gay life" as the liberation movement was to demand, more a plea for fairness. A positive step, yet it was a middle class protest against the de-legitimisation of the law – one of the pillars of a society they wanted to save.

Another sign of progress was a *Sydney Morning Herald* opinion piece of 1967 which declared that homosexuality was neither a crime, nor a disease, but rather "a condition that has brought, because of the sanctions against it, unnecessary suffering to about one man in every twenty and has brought to society at large a multitude of evils – deceit, blackmail, suicide and disease."[16]

Gays themselves started to talk publicly about law reform. An organiser of what was described as Australia's first ever homosexual ball told the tabloid *Impact*, that "the Ball's profits would finance a campaign to have homosexual acts between males – now legal in Britain – made legal in Australia."[17]

Even earlier though, homosexuals were starting to be heard, albeit somewhat anonymously. In 1963, in the first survey that included "healthy" lesbians and homosexual men (usually people in prison or psychiatric hospitals were studied), the University of Adelaide student union canvassed students' sexual experiences and published the results in *On Dit*. A similar survey was carried out at Queensland University in 1965 and reported in *Semper Floreat*.[18]

Five hundred students crowded the Melbourne University Debating Society's forum on homosexual law reform in July 1964. Putting the case for reform were students Patrick McCaughy, Gareth Evans and court psychiatrist A A Bartholomew, while those against were law lecturer Clifford Pannam and students Michael Redfern and Peter Carter. The focus was on 'individual freedom' and whose morality should predominate. Those against reform were the most questioned and the yes vote at the end was an overwhelming 281:98.[19]

1964 was the first year an article from a self-proclaimed homosexual appeared anywhere in Australia. In Monash University's student newspaper *Lots Wife*, under the title "The Homosexual Villain", an unnamed first year student stated "The fact is, of course, that in itself, homosexuality is no more unnatural than masturbation." France and Italy had "turned away from the barbarity of Christian morality" and decriminalised homosexuality under the Napoleonic Code, while the Anglo-Saxon sphere had criminalised homosexuality for over a hundred years. What right, this student asked, had the state to interfere with private arrangements made by two adult individuals? The response was largely positive.[20]

Censorship became a student issue. Gerster and Bassett in their book on the sixties ignore the decades-long fight of the Communist Party against censorship, but they document the new role of the student activists. "In an age of slogans, *Make Love not War* is among the most enduring...The student press...led the charge against 'bourgeois morality'." Publishing excerpts from prohibited literature, student papers "embarked on a prolonged campaign of guerrilla warfare against censorship." *Thorunka* published one of English poet WH Auden's long suppressed and "graphically homosexual" poems as well as excerpts from *Eskimo Nell*. Editors such as *Thorunka*'s Wendy Bacon found themselves before the courts, but the authorities seemed "virtually powerless to check the inroads such publications were making into censorship".[21]

At the same time, however, the federal government suddenly stepped up its scrutiny, specifically targeting gays in its employ. The trigger for this move was primarily the fallout from a British spy case, involving blackmail of John Vassall, Naval Attache to Moscow. It created panic in the UK and Australia, apparently more for governments being caught unawares than out of homosexual paranoia.[22]

But some warned of the homosexual "threat". ASIO head Sir Charles Spry told Prime Minister Menzies that homosexuals constituted "a most serious risk to the security of the Commonwealth".[23]

Spry worried about a close knit "homintern" (a play on the Soviet Comintern) that was loyal only to its members. He recommended that homosexuals be tightly vetted and strictly monitored if employed and that it be done with much discretion. For the first time lesbians were formally included in anti-gay provisions, "... the security risks which derive from homosexual practices are considered to apply equally to women..." Lesbians, especially in the armed forces, had been discussed earlier and Spry's report cited an unnamed Coffee Shop in Wellington Street, St Kilda as being a well-known rendezvous for military personnel. As histories of lesbian life in Melbourne record, these women were very well aware of police surveillance and there was a well-organised escape route if customers at the front of the cafe spotted the police, civilian or military.[24]

Spry and his supporters didn't exactly get the crackdown they wanted. After a year considering the request, the Public Service Board agreed only to "discreet surveillance" of public sector staff by the Commonwealth Police. Given that there were already state police, vice squad and ASIO lists of suspected homosexuals, it's possible the Board considered there was already enough surveillance. No star chamber McCarthyite witchhunts were to occur in Australia, even though homosexuals were victimised, sacked, denied promotion or appointment because of all this surveillance activity. But these days of widespread discrimination and victimisation were numbered.

America – from Cold War to Stonewall

America too was emerging from the Cold War climate. The early 1960s saw a number of significant court wins for homosexuals on the right to work, distribution of homosexual publications, as well as curbing police harassment. The first signs of increased confidence to speak out publicly came on 19 September 1964 when members of the New York League for Sexual Freedom picketed the Whitehall Induction Centre in New York, in protest at the military's anti-lesbian and anti-homosexual employment policies.

The next year there were more demonstrations. On April 17 outside the UN, ten gays protested the sending of homosexuals to labour camps in Cuba. They carried placards saying "Cuba's government persecutes gays, US government beat them to it." Then at the White House, first with ten protesters on May 29, then thirty-five on 23 October, demonstrators demanded job security in government employment. A Philadelphia protest occurred on 4 July, highlighting the lack of constitutional rights. The Pentagon was a target on July 31 and then the State Department on August 28, as gays again protested discrimination in the military. Six demonstrations in one year![25]

But there was another, a seventh, and the biggest for 1965. One of the few all-night venues, a Dewey restaurant in central Philadelphia, regularly refused service to young people who were mostly black, "homosexuals and persons wearing non-conformist clothing". The young people organised a sit-in, the police were called, some were arrested and then found guilty of disorderly conduct. The local homophile organisation, the Janus Society, helped organise a further protest. 150 leafleted outside Dewey's, continuing the action for five days. A second sit-in a week later saw the police called, but no-one was arrested. As Marc Stein reports it, "An hour later the protesters declared victory and they left the restaurant".[26]

We are used to citing 1969 and Stonewall, but for homosexuals in the US, 1965 was really the year that everything began to change.

A number of protests turned into one-off riots outside bars and other social venues in the lead up to 1969. They were inspired by the black riots sweeping the country as Belinda Baldwin notes: "Along with the rest of the country, gay Americans watched as the Civil Rights Movement evolved from the polite marches in the 1950's to the angry protests of the 60's..." [27]

In 1966 Los Angeles Black Cat Tavern patrons were arrested for "kissing in" the New Year. It ignited a riot, which spiraled across the street, with the police then raiding another bar, beating up the owner and knocking two bar staff unconscious. Those who went to trial were convicted, something that could have demoralized the community. Instead PRIDE, a community-based civil defence group, held a successful protest rally on February 11. These actions had a major impact on the ways lesbians and homosexuals viewed themselves. As Baldwin concludes, gays were standing up for their rights across the country and they "were beginning to feel as if they had the right to assemble in peace, and that it was the police who were in the wrong".

Then came 1969 and the riot at New York's Stonewall Inn.

Over five days from June 27 the crowds gathered, marched and chanted slogans such as "Gay Power!", while bricks and bottles went flying through the air at police. And with these words ringing out, the world witnessed the riotous birth of a new radical movement – Gay Liberation.

A *Village Voice* reporter walking back from the last night of the protests in July 1969 with gay poet Allen Ginsberg, wrote these prophetic words: "As Ginsberg turned to head toward home, he waved and yelled, 'Defend the fairies!'... Watch out. The liberation is under way."

Jim Fourratt recalled that "The next day, a group of us got together and we organized the Gay Liberation Front. That was the importance of Stonewall." Fourratt may not have known about the Black Cat riot and the continuing protests, but the activists in New York recognised the same political imperatives. What *was* new was that gays were no longer prepared to accept tolerance or reform measures. "We wanted fundamental change", Fourrat declared.[28]

Leaflets began circulating round Greenwich Village and surrounds, calling for a meeting and further action. Provocatively titled *Do you think homosexuals are revolting? You bet your sweet ass we are*, the leaflet went on "We're going to make a place for ourselves in the revolutionary movement. We challenge the myths that are screwing up this society."[29]

Gay Liberation had entered the political arena. It was determined to fight on all fronts, arguing that "We identify ourselves with all the oppressed: the Vietnamese struggle, the third world, the blacks, the workers, the women...all those oppressed by this rotten, dirty, vile, fucked-up capitalist conspiracy."[30]

Australia – the beginnings

Although influenced by Stonewall and the radicalization of the times, Australian gays didn't immediately form Gay Liberation groups. The first "gay rights" organisation (but not a gay organisation) began in July 1969 in Canberra. The Homosexual Law Reform Society arose in response to a new Draft Criminal Code for the Territory, which, with additions included by the federal government, actually made things worse for homosexuals. The group while a positive step, folded before any change to the laws in the ACT occurred.[31] Other attempts to set up similar groups interstate during 1969 and 1970, usually through the Humanist Society, faltered very early on. While the Society and other civil liberties groups continued to support the call for reform, it was homosexuals themselves whose campaigns won law reform.[32]

But before gays got organised, women took to protesting. Women's Liberation burst onto the Australian scene on 21 October 1969, when CPA member Zelda D'Aprano chained herself to front doors of Government offices in Melbourne calling for equal pay. She was joined in a second protest by Alva Geikie and Thelma Solomon. This action was the start of the Women's Action Committee, the first Australian Women's Liberation group.[33]

In Sydney, after meetings of a dozen women, the Women's Liberation Movement declared itself at the December 15 anti-Vietnam War demonstration. Arguing that "Only the chains have changed", their leaflet linked women's struggle with that of the Vietnamese people and explained why the roots of their oppression lay within the capitalist system.[34]

From the beginning, the Australian WLM was heavily influenced by left-wing ideas and included women from the left organisations. The New Left was important in the early days of WLM, but Sue Wills shows that for Sydney Women's Liberation, most of the women from the left were in the CPA.[35]

This is reflected in the early publications, a leaflet in January 1970 acknowledging that "the ideas and reasoning behind women's liberation reflect traditional themes of the radical socialist left" and explicitly located women's liberation within 1960s radicalism. Sydney WL wrote "There is an increasing self-awareness on the part of the powerless and the manipulated of all societies. Third world struggles against imperialism, black demands for power, student demands for shared control of the university, rank and file workers' opposition to union bureaucrats as well as bosses and community demands for control of environment all share the same idea of combating particular repressions and injustices where they occur. And the same goes for Women's Liberation."[36]

Participants saw the movement as strengthening the left. Sue Wills says they believed "the concepts of oppression and exploitation could be applied to an analysis of the position of women from which followed that 'women's liberation advocates solutions similar to the rest of the socialist movement'." Women's Liberation and the radicalisation of women around the demands of the movement drew thousands into action and impacted the lives of many, many more.[37]

Amongst these were lesbians. For many it was the first indication that women could organise and fight for their rights, especially on the job. And lesbians who joined Women's Liberation looked to "their" movement to fight for them too. However there were obstacles, even within WLM. While the movement did take up lesbian demands, there was some early reluctance. In the US a group of lesbians invaded one conference, displaying their T-shirts which bore the slogan "Lavender Menace". They then addressed the assembled women calling on them to support lesbian demands.[38] There were a few confrontations in Australia, most notably at the Women and Theory conference in January 1973, when a group of lesbians from Hobart challenged WLM to deal with the exclusion or denigration of lesbians within its ranks.[39]

Catalysts for Change - ALM

In Australia at the same time Women's Liberation started, two lesbians formed the first openly homosexual political group, the Australasian Lesbian Movement (ALM). It attracted the first of those who wanted change.[40] Its politics, however, were closer to those of the American Daughters of Bilitis than Women's Liberation, calling for acceptance and reform rather than liberation. Sitting on the cusp of change, a reformist organisation at a time when revolution was in the air, the ALM was contradictory. It came into being as a brave first step for homosexuals organising in this country: on the one hand radical in its openness, drawing in a number of lesbians, calling themselves a *movement*; but on the other hand, gaining membership primarily amongst lesbians seeking a social group, who didn't want the political activism, didn't in fact want the public exposure.

ALM initially did focus on public engagement by lesbians themselves with wider society, a determination to break down prejudice and discrimination. They presented a public face to the world, whether it was in the press or television, a meeting space and contact phone, breaking the silence. Francesca Curtis was the first open homosexual on Australian television (in fact in any media). Interviewed by Channel 9's late night Bailey File in June 1970, she talked about her life, the possibilities for change and why the ALM had been set up.

Soon after the initial burst of publicity, ALM published an information sheet outlining their history and aims, a combination of caution and optimism:

> "It would be idealistic to think that we, in our lifetime, will see a great change in public attitudes to Lesbianism. However, we can hope that television and radio programmes such as the ones in which we have been involved will do something towards showing people what we are like and will thus help them to understand and accept us. More familiarity with the word "Lesbian" and an accurate definition of the word – something our publicity is at least supplying – could be in itself enough to correct many misconceptions about us."[41]

But there were other, younger and more left wing activists who were starting to organise, responding to the radicalism of the time. "The present mood", as commentator Malcolm Mackerras observed "is one of adventure, not of caution."[42]

Phyllis Papps, a leader of ALM recalls that, "A lot happened during what was basically a very short period of time. You had things like Germaine Greer writing her book, *The Female Eunuch*. You had the Labor Party coming into power after 23 years in the wilderness...Things happening in the US that had a huge impact here, such as the race riots and Stonewall... In 1970 Jim Cairns led 70,000 in Melbourne streets opposing the Vietnam War. Women's libbers were out in the streets, protests about male domination in unions, protests against racism. There was an incredible minefield of issues that were being built on."[43]

ALM responded to the increasing radicalisation at first by shifting towards a more political stance, but then some in the group shied away, pulling the group in a more socially oriented direction. Instead of arguing for ALM to embrace the emerging culture, many in the group concluded that further change was not possible. Even after Australia's first homosexual demonstration, the newsletter's editorial said "We must however face up to the cold reality. Australia is hardly the place for any world-shattering reforms... To spend time on a society that is more disinterested than scornful, is time wasted. So what do we do? We make the most of what we have. A club that provides a meeting place for Lesbians, a newsletter that provides a contact for those of us who are otherwise isolated."[44] As a political group ALM did not survive the tumultuous days of the early 1970s, never breaking out of its base in Melbourne, despite attracting some interstate membership. It became instead a long-running social group, catering to the shy or discreet lesbian.

Nonetheless Phyllis Papps and Francesca Curtis could truthfully claim, "We were the forerunners...for others to follow on... the catalysts for change."[45]

"We came of age politically" - CAMP

The mantle of political activism had already been taken up by another group – a combined lesbian and male homosexual group - Campaign Against Moral Persecution or CAMP.

After reading about Gay Liberation and the actions of gays in the US, in mid-1970 one Sydney University psychology student found himself sitting in a lecture theatre, hearing how aversion therapy, a particularly barbaric "treatment" could cure him of his homosexuality. Not that anyone in the lecture theatre knew he was gay, but inside he was seething. That night he met up with his next door neighbour, a fellow homosexual and by the end of the night, they agreed, "Stuff it, let's do it". So it was that Christabel Poll and John Ware decided to start a homosexual rights group in Sydney. John Ware recalls their initial low-key aims, "We had the notion that this would be a society of half a dozen people who would meet once a month or so and keep our presence in the public eye by publishing letters to the editor and challenging statements that came out... Really a sort of book club..."[46]

A second meeting, including members of NSW Council for Civil Liberties, established that the group could legally meet, a real concern given male homosexuality was still criminalised. The name Campaign Against Moral Persecution or CAMP was adopted and then they took their first political action, a letter to the newspapers. The letter stated that homosexuals were "good citizens and contribute much to society" and they resented their treatment as "freaks, mental defectives, dangerous perverts or all three".

While the letter was published in a couple of outlets, it had no significant impact until *The Australian* interviewed Poll and Ware. In a two-page spread, entitled "Couples" in September 1970, homosexuals "came out" nationally in the Australian media. Not as the "freaks or perverts" but the very "normal and ordinary" next-door neighbor type of people.[47] Commenting on the increasing coverage, welcome as it was, Paul Foss noted that earlier articles had been patronizing. Reportage of the formation of CAMP "indicated that something new had occurred... homosexuals were willing to avow their sexuality in public – 'come out'... and to reject an apologetic platform".[48]

It was a watershed moment.

"The response was absolutely amazing" Ware remembers. "Letters poured in". After going through the several hundred responses, a smaller number were selected to invite to a combined BBQ and get-together on 21 November 1970 in Sydney. Within a few months the group had spread to most state capitals and by the end of 1971, the campuses.

The group's first priority was to publish a magazine to provide a forum for ideas, amongst homosexuals to begin with and then outward to the wider society. Its second aim was to set up a legal, medical and employment advice centre, along with a legal defence fund. In this it was very similar to ALM.

Only in the third goal mentioned was anything resembling a public campaign and that was just a brief "agitate for law reform".

Still CAMP was a more politicized group than ALM. Its strengths were its mixed membership, its openness to younger, radicalizing homosexuals (ALM had a 21-year age limit) and the fact that it had to deal with the illegality of male homosexuality. The latter forced the group to take a more political stance and build campaigns.

Initially they were not prepared to go beyond the mildest of actions. Christabel Poll penned a page-long article which distanced CAMP from Gay Liberation style militancy. She admitted the goal of a better understanding of homosexuality and a redefinition of homosexual's place in the community was "hardly a stirring call to militant action". She believed CAMP's aim of building as broad a movement as possible would not be furthered by militancy.[49]

CAMP Ink's Editorial for January 1971 supported this stand: "We do not advocate that homosexuals in Australia should immediately march down the street carrying GL placards, but we do feel that it should be recognised by all homosexuals that it is a necessary step to be taken eventually – maybe not for 20 years – but we must now work towards the day when we can walk down the street openly as homosexuals."

But like ALM, CAMP had no control over the pace of events. The radical mood of the times encouraged political demonstrations and gays who'd joined in the rallies against the Vietnam War, gone on strike or joined the Freedom Rides, as well as lesbians influenced by the newly formed Women's Liberation, wanted more radical responses. Even as CAMP formed it was being superseded, particularly on the campuses. At Sydney University, lecturer Dennis Altman who'd been involved in the GLF in America and had just published one of the first books on Gay Liberation, encouraged greater militancy.

By July 1971, just six months after CAMP started meeting at Sydney University, a Gay Liberation "cell" had formed within Campus CAMP. Initially a discussion group, it politically outgrew its founding organisation and in October Gay Lib formally split, but not before CAMP found itself on the street in Australia's first gay demonstration.

In 1970 Federal Attorney-General Tom Hughes had raised the possibility of law reform, suggesting that "homosexual acts should not necessarily be within the ambit of criminal law". His suggestion had been welcomed by editorials in the *Canberra Times* and *The Age*. Sixteen months later Hughes was challenged for Liberal Party preselection. While he had effectively withdrawn his support for change soon after he raised it, CAMP thought he was still amenable to persuasion and definitely didn't want to see the other candidate, the open homophobe Jim Cameron, displace Hughes.

On the night of the preselection, 6 October 1971, 70 CAMP members and supporters gathered outside Liberal Party Headquarters in Sydney. It was both serious and fun. The protesters were scared and defiant, holding up banners announcing their homosexuality and demands for equality. They handed out a leaflet about CAMP's position on the candidates and gave away some of their 150 politically inscribed balloons. All the while they were chanting "Hughes In, Cameron Out" and "2,4,6,8, Gay's just as good as straight". It was reported that those inside the building could hear the chants and songs.

They'd done it – protested and chanted years before CAMP's founders dreamed it was possible. One participant talked afterwards of the camaraderie, "of the feeling that you were actually doing something". Two lesbians carried their placard "I am lesbian and I am beautiful", on the bus to the demo, drawing inquisitive stares. At the demo two young men high-kicked behind their bright pink "Queens" banner. Bringing the protest to an end the balloons, with their gay rights slogans were released and the crowd sang a rousing rendition of "God bless Australia's Queens".[50]

None of the mainstream press covered it, but Channel 9 showed the protest on the late news and that week's *Bulletin* noted its occurrence, alongside its article about the preselection entitled "A helping hand from CAMP". Hughes had won the ballot.[51]

It was, as *Camp Ink* said "the month...when we came of age politically".[52]

But this was also the month when CAMP passed its peak. The organisation itself lasted many years afterwards. Its members were often side by side with Gay Liberation in the protests and forums to push for lesbian and gay rights. But the mantle for the struggle had been passed to Gay Liberation.

Chapter 4

Gay Liberation. The Age of Demonstrations[1]

The early days were exciting. A time, when gays "came out" and hit the streets in mass shows of defiance, anger and pride. It was a movement, activist Craig Johnston wrote, that "attracted the imagination of the homosexual youth...defining for most people what homosexual radicalism meant."

Gay is Good!

The 1960s radicalisation changed everything for the left. Around the world it broke the stranglehold of the Cold War, drew in millions to the anti-Vietnam War movement and saw the rise of the New Left, as well as the radical movements. In all these areas young lesbians and gay men were present, demanding fundamental change and asking themselves, why weren't they marching for their own liberation?

In 1969, exploding on the streets of New York, came just the movement for them – Gay Liberation. Dennis Altman wrote about the changed consciousness it gave rise to: "Gay is angry, gay is proud, and homosexuals are no longer apologising for being what they are."[2] Martha Shelley's iconic article *Gay is Good* had put it more dramatically: "Look out, straights. Here comes the Gay Liberation Front, springing up like warts all over the bland face of Amerika...We are your worst fears made flesh... we are the sort of people everyone was taught to despise – and now we are shaking off the chains of self-hatred and marching on your citadels of repression."[3]

GLF had marked a sharp political break with past activism. Not that homosexuals had been invisible or inactive. In the early 1960s, as we've seen, there had been public demonstrations of homosexuals against employment discrimination, police harassment of gay bars and the like. This activism, however, had rarely gone past one-off protests or the call for modest reform of the system.

The difference is highlighted by Sherry Wolf. "What separated the Stonewall Riots from all previous gay activism was not merely the unexpected nights-long defiance in the streets, but the conscious mobilization in the riot's wake of new and seasoned activists who gave expression to this more militant mood."[4]

Among the more experienced were some from the socialist organisations, but also many from the established homophile groups the Mattachine Society and Daughters of Bilitis (DOB). These groups had been the ones to call the first protest rally immediately after the riots. Martha Shelly, on behalf of DOB, recalls going to a meeting of Mattachine and putting the proposal for a march to the people there – around 400 of them – and "I don't think anybody's hand stayed down. Everybody wanted to do it." Mattachine and DOB then put an ad in the *Village Voice* calling a rally for early July.[5]

The newly formed Gay Liberation Front snatched the initiative in the fight for gay rights from Mattachine and DOB. Subsequent rallies which pulled out thousands of lesbians and gay men were organised by the GLF, as DOB and Mattachine drew back from the new, confrontational movement. Influenced by socialist ideas, the GLF put a more left-wing ideology to the fore. Although few were Marxists and many of the publications didn't spell out a clear politics, GLF adopted the language of "revolution", rather than the earlier agenda of winning acceptance within existing society. As Jim Fourratt, a founder of GLF said, "There was going to be a revolution, and we were going to be a part of it."[6]

GLF also linked its cause with other oppressed groups, telling the underground paper *Rat*:

"We are a revolutionary homosexual group of men and women formed with the realization that complete sexual liberation for all people cannot come about unless existing social institutions are abolished. We reject society's attempt to impose sexual roles and definitions of our nature.... We identify ourselves with all the oppressed: the Vietnamese struggle, the third world, the blacks, the workers...all those oppressed by this rotten, dirty, vile, fucked-up capitalist conspiracy."[7]

Australia – Gay Lib comes to town

Gay Liberation (GLM) was the last of the radical movements to appear on the Australian political scene. The Stonewall riots themselves did not rate a mention in the Australian press in 1969, though it's clear a number of gays in Australia knew about the American events and were soon to begin organising themselves.

Dennis Altman, who'd spent time in an American Gay Liberation group brought their ideas back with him. Writing in the "Family Issue" of *Tharunka*, Altman said Gay Liberation was more than changing the laws. "Unlike the old line homophile movements, GL sees with Marx that the liberation of each depends on the liberation of all and has thus sought to build alliances with other oppressed groups. For the homosexual cannot win liberation without a general sexual liberation, one that will move far beyond the much vaunted 'permissive society' to a genuine release of our erotic and loving instincts which are held back by the repression necessary for the maintenance of our repressive and inhuman 'civilization'."[8]

However for a time the only openly gay groups around were the reformist groups such as CAMP and ALM and anyone wanting to fight for gay rights joined them; in the case of many lesbians, bringing with them the radical ideas of Women's Liberation.[9]

In the early days CAMP publications did carry articles espousing the ideas of Gay Liberation. Society Five, the Melbourne branch of CAMP told the Melbourne University student paper *Farrago* in April 1971 that gay liberation would entail not only the liberation of homosexuals, but would lead to the liberation of all people.

But the two groups had very different approaches. Gay Liberation's aims were revolutionary change, not reform of the system and their tactics prioritised mass actions rather than lobbying. While there was obviously overlap (the new militants wanted the laws against male homosexuals repealed just as much as the reformists), how you won change and how much change you wanted, was *the* question. Oppression, resistance, liberation was the language that marked out the GLM's demands for change and its character as a movement influenced by Marxism.

Some in CAMP repudiated Gay Liberation, distancing themselves from politics "styled on the American liberationist movements, of which Gay Power is a specimen". One student at Sydney University argued that adopting such politics would narrow the aims of gay rights groups and alienate the broader membership; despite the fact that Gay Liberation in the US had brought tens of thousands of new people into gay activism.[10]

Against the more working class and left wing demands of Gay Liberation, others called for a movement that looked to more general social reforms. In one of the earliest articles in the student press, "Why Gay Liberation?" the first line was "Gay, Gay, Gay – is there another way?" It argued that instead of a being a despised minority, homosexuals had political potential. "A minority group, confused and fragmented, but surely a powerful front if ever united because it draws people from all levels of society." The article went on, however, to make clear it wasn't for revolution. It focussed instead on the value of homosexuals to current society. The idea of drawing people from all levels of society meant there could be no argument for fundamental social change, just better consideration of homosexuals in today's world. Even their suggestion to have a gay contingent on an anti-war march was to prove the extent that homosexuals were committed to others.[11]

While students formed the first Gay Liberation group at Sydney University, it was the organised Left which first promoted the GLF's revolutionary politics, before the group had appeared.

Denis Freney's article "Gay Liberation" appeared on 26 May 1971. Freney reminded his readers that after the Russian Revolution the Bolshelviks had repealed anti-homosexual laws, while also detailing the impact of Stalinism in turning back the gains of the revolution. Outlining the rise of the GLF in America, he discussed its links with Women's Liberation and the Black and anti-Vietnam War struggles. He called for the radical left to "give every aid to the movement for liberation of the gays" and to support sexual freedom.[12]

Gay Liberation began in Australia as a radical "cell" of CAMP at Sydney University in July 1971. Two Women's Liberationists started it as a consciousness-raising group discussing both personal experience and political analysis. Soon around ten women and men were attending, some coming after hearing Dennis Altman address meetings on his recent experiences in the US. The group's main focus turned to discussing feminist and left-wing gay liberation theories and literature. John Lee recalls that in 1971 he and then partner Tony Crewes were very interested in "sexual liberation in the most radical form"; reading Germaine Greer and Kate Millett's *Sexual Politics*, as well as books such as Marcuse's *Eros and Civilization*. But it was seeing reports of demonstrations in the US in magazines like *Gay Sunshine*, celebrating the second anniversary of the Stonewall riots that fired them up. With US protest slogans such as "We're Fairies and We're Fighting", the pair "completely identified with this American style of gay liberation". Confrontational actions such as kiss-ins on Sydney trains, "was the style of what we took to be gay liberation politics. We weren't into writing letters or negotiating with ministers".[13]

Towards the end of 1971 CAMP and the Gay Liberation cell could no longer co-exist as a single organisation, even though CAMP had become more open and militant after organising Australia's first demonstration in October 1971. While the groups did join forces on occasions afterwards, fundamental political differences had split them. The call in the first editorial of *CAMP Ink*, for example, for "the right to serve our country without fear of exposure and contempt", was unlikely to be shared by those opposed to the war in Vietnam or who rejected incorporation into present-day society.[14]

Gay Lib "came out" at the Sex Lib forum at Sydney University on 19 January 1972, where Germaine Greer, Gillian Leahy from Women's Liberation, Liz Fell (Libertarian) and Dennis Altman gave their views on the liberation movements. Referring to the banners around the room as well as people leafletting, Dennis delighted in "outing" the new Gay Lib forces. "As they have now identified themselves by the process of exhibitionism, which as we all know, is the hallmark of homosexuals, you will of course be aware that Gay Liberation has come out not only in Sydney but also in Australia."[15]

Like CAMP before it, Gay Liberation quickly spread, with groups in every major capital except Perth by the end of 1972.[16] The Adelaide University student paper *On Dit* reported that 350 people turned up on 23 August 1972 to hear Dennis Altman and students Lex Watson and Jill Mathews. After the speakers, Jill asked those not interested in Gay Liberation (described by Dennis as being "primarily for homosexuals") to leave. Around 100 people stayed, making it Adelaide's first GLM meeting.[17] For the first time high school students formed openly gay groups; four in 1972, including the all-boys Fort Street High School.[18]

Early on Gay Lib spelt out its aims and what distinguished it from groups such as CAMP. Melbourne's *Gay Rays* wrote, "Our position in society is ratshit. Limited reform will not improve this position much because it cannot alter deeply rooted social attitudes which oppress us in so many ways. Working towards law reform and forming a cozy social ghetto within society is accepting the values that have oppressed us."[19]

Activism was the first step in revolutionary change. *Gay Rays* quoted the Gay Liberation Manifesto: "The sexual revolution is a continuous process... Gay Liberation sees the most important first step towards change as the development of pride and self-assurance in being a homosexual. We need to fight self-oppression and gain a sense of community, otherwise we can achieve nothing." This was the consciousness raising adopted from WLM, that involved many in the early days. But lesbians and gays had to hit outwards at oppressive institutions, not focus on individual change. "By activism, eg, demonstrations, leafleting, etc, Gay Liberation seeks not benign tolerance and handouts from society but confrontation to demand our rights. This shows society we exist and at last are not afraid to fight."[20]

Gay Liberation declared itself against sexism. A leaflet introducing the GLM to new members wrote, "As we cannot carry out this revolutionary change alone and as the abolition of the family and gender is also a necessary condition of Women's Liberation, we will work to form a strategic alliance with Women's Liberation Movement, aiming to develop our ideas and our practice in close interrelation." [21]

Just announcing a commonality of oppression didn't end sexism. It was to prove an ongoing area of contention, within CAMP and Gay Liberation, leading to splits within the movement as many lesbians refused to keep working with gay men.[22] Instances of sexism encouraged the adoption of radical feminist and then avowedly lesbian separatist politics, though a rightward shifting political milieu was the major reason radical feminism became hegemonic. The shift towards separatism also weakened Gay Liberation and made it harder for leftist gays to argue the case for socialist politics.

Nonetheless there were many joint actions during 1972 and 1973, including the first Gay Lib demo. ABC TV had cut a segment about Dennis Altman and his path-breaking book *Homosexual: oppression and liberation*. In Melbourne a group of about a dozen protestors gathered outside the station's studios, chanting "2,4,6,8, Gay is just as good as straight; 3,5,7,9 Try it our way just one time".[23]

Sydney's demonstration was equally colourful, but bigger with around 80-100 protesting. It was here that the first arrest for political homosexual activism, rather than for the "crime" of the sexual act, was made. A protester carrying the placard "We're not fucked up, we're fucked over" was arrested for "unseemly language".[24]

Gay Liberation. The Age of Demonstrations

A couple of weeks after the demo came Sex Lib week. At Sydney Town Hall a speaker announced, "Whether you like it or not – we are inadvertently part of the revolution. And it's growing stronger by the minute. We are there with the dope smokers and Women's Lib – with the black minorities and the Jews. We are a minority and we are oppressed... There's a revolution taking place and we are at the centre. Get involved. Power to the People."[25]

As symbols of oppression, both the Catholic and Anglican churches came under fire, though some of the protestant churches had supported homosexual law reform during the 1960s. The Anglican Church was the first target. Two gay couples appeared on ABC TV's Chequerboard in December 1972, resulting in the sacking of one of them, Peter Bonsall-Boone, even though church officials already knew he was gay. Gay Lib and CAMP demonstrated outside church offices. Peter de Waal, Bonsall-Boone's partner was backed by his union in case of a similar threat of losing his job.[26]

Equally a target was the psychiatric profession which administered aversion therapy, lobotomy and other barbarities. A number of psychiatrists were based on Sydney campuses, with one particularly notorious individual, Neil McConaghy at Sydney University. One zap (a stunt) involved gays hurling eggs at McConaghy as he tried to justify his treatment regime. Protesters handed out leaflets to 250 participants in the "Psychiatry and Liberation" conference, where he was speaking, pointing out why they were "not prepared to come along and 'rationally' debate our position with our oppressors".[27]

Street theatre, forums and zaps targeted many psychiatric conferences, finally forcing the psychiatrists' and psychologists' professional bodies to adopt policies that no longer classed gays as "sick" or "deviant".[28]

"One good zap is worth six months on the psychiatrist's couch. One hour on the streets screaming and proclaiming your homosexuality is worth six hundred hours in a consciousness-raising group" was the verdict on Australian gays "largest demo ever" on

Melbourne's streets in December 1972. Around 300 gays gave Melbourne's busy shoppers a "unique treat" by handing out "homosexual apples", parading in the city centre and dancing around with big, glitter-covered letters spelling out *Love, Homosexual* and *Gay Liberation*. It pulled people away from the traditional Myer Christmas windows and "lit up the faces of shoppers".[29]

"Coming out" – being visible – was a mainstay of Gay Lib. The GLF leaflet advertising the December action said the demonstration was organised to "assert the fact that homosexuals exist in the community. Gay Lib is a group of homosexuals who are open about their homosexuality...Showing ourselves in public is a step in creating confidence..."[30]

Joining forces with other oppressed groups was important for Gay Liberation. Sydney's IWD in 1972 was an historic event, marking the first time the Gay Liberation banner "Gay Liberation – Come Out" had appeared in public, with about 40 in a combined Gay Lib and CAMP contingent.[31] In 1972 Melbourne gays marched in the 30 June Moratorium, while Sydney Gay Liberation marched under its own banner at the anti-Vietnam war march on 20 January 1973.[32]

Pink bans

Discrimination at work was an ever-present issue. A first for working class solidarity were bans, now known as "Pink Bans", put on by the NSW branch of the Builders Labourers Federation (BLF) in support of two gay students.

In June 1973, student and Gay Lib club treasurer Jeremy Fisher was expelled from a Church of England residential college at Macquarie University. Told by the college head Alan Cole that homosexuality was a perversion, he had to agree to "be chaste" and accept treatment or he'd be out. Fisher refused and took his case, somewhat hesitantly, to a couple office bearers in the student union. Rod Webb, editor of the student newspaper *Arena*, a member of the Socialist Workers League (SWL) and Jeff Hayler, Chair of the Students Representative Council (SRC), took up his case straight away. They organised some on-campus rallies and as Fisher recalls they immediately went to work, ringing their contacts across Sydney. The ABC interviewed him and showed the footage on that night's news. "Suddenly the Builders' Labourers' Federation (BLF) had green-banned construction at the college over me."[33]

Buildings were being put up apace at Macquarie, including the residences that Fisher was staying at. The union had gone to its members and put the request for support to them. They had voted that if Jeremy Fisher wasn't reinstated then building would stop, not only at the college but on other sites at the university.[34]

At one point it looked like the whole deal would unravel, as Jeremy Fisher tells the story:

> "The BLF assumed I wanted to go back until one day, back down in the Students' Council basement, Bob Pringle, then part of the BLF's leadership, asked me:
> "Why do you want to go back into that place?"
> "I don't," I said.
> "But we're out on strike to put you back," he said, a hint of anger in his eyes.
> "I thought because I'd been kicked out because I was gay," I answered.
> Bob paused then said: "I guess you're right. It's the principle of the thing. They shouldn't pick on a bloke because of his sexuality."

Jack Mundey, NSW secretary of the union and a member of the CPA, explained that "the homosexual movement had come to the Builders' Labourers and said, you're against the idea of workers not having a right, well [it's the same for students not having rights]." Because the students and workers had joined forces against the Vietnam War and anti-apartheid, Mundey said, there was already a sense of solidarity between students and trade unionists. Not that every builders labourer was "a galloping conservationist or women's libber or even supporter of the rights of gays", Mundey pointed out, but the union encouraged people from the various campaigns and liberation movements to address members about discrimination.

Jeremy Fisher paid tribute. "It was a brave decision for a union to take. It wasn't popular with members, though the principle that people should be free to express their sexuality was grudgingly accepted."

Later that year, again at Macquarie, teacher trainee Penny Short lost her scholarship for publishing an explicit lesbian poem. When the department refused to reinstate the scholarship, the Teachers Federation official Cathy MacDonald pledged the support of the union and the BLF threatened to stop work at Macquarie. Fellow student teachers who had a campaign going for better allowances and conditions backed her at one of their mass meetings and joined a demonstration outside the Education Department.[35]

While gays in Brisbane marched for the first time on May Day 1973,[36] Sydney's May Day march of that year wasn't a cause for celebration for Gay Liberation – but there was a successful zap called by Women's Liberation. Women and gays refused to join the May Day procession in protest at the "Miss May Day" competition. At the end rallying point they handed out leaflets and demanded a say on the platform. When they were denied speaking rights they stormed the platform and started addressing the crowd. The crowd applauded, but the organisers accused them of being violent. Craig Johnston countered that the oppressed had the right to fight back, speaking of "Gay Liberation tactics – open angry, defiant, proud militancy."[37]

Theories and activism

It wasn't all street marches during Gay Liberation's first years. Almost every radical group during the 60s and 70s had its own Manifesto describing the oppression of the capitalist state and arguing how to bring about change. Gay Lib here was no exception; but it adopted the London GLF's version rather than fashioning its own. The London Manifesto prefaced its demands saying, "Before we can create the new society of the future we have to defend our interests as gay people here and now..." Consequently the Manifesto called for an end to discrimination at work, sex education that recognised the validity of homosexuality and an end to police harassment and psychiatric treatment.

These were demands on society. The Manifesto concluded: "We do not intend to ask for anything. We intend to stand firm and assert our basic rights. If this involves violence it will not be we who initiate this, but those who attempt to stand in our way to freedom."[38]

Debate about activism and theory were part of the development of Gay Liberation. At the beginning of 1973, 80 gays collected at the Communist Party camp, Minto, a mixed bunch of labourers, seamen, university lecturers, high school and uni students as well as old age pensioners. Papers by Dennis Altman and Pam Stein were a call to radically restructure society, while Barry Prothero and Lance Gowland discussed "Vanguard group or mass group?" and relations with the left, especially the CPA.[39]

Despite the successful activities, by its second year Gay Liberation was struggling to maintain itself, numbers at meetings were declining, the finances were in a parlous state and there was questioning of the usefulness of some protests. GLM's decline was not just a localised problem. Rather it was a function of the failure of the world-wide upsurge that had given rise to the liberation movements, though it took longer to have an impact in Australia.

The group tried many strategies to stay functioning. Suggestions as early as January 1973 called for an activities group "whose job will be to organise campaigns and actions which have popular support amongst our members." CPA member Lance Gowland said the group should be zapping more psychiatrists and anti-gay film showings, holding demonstrations against job discrimination and a national conference.[40]

But nothing seemed to work and by the middle of 1973 "pissed off activists" called a meeting "to clarify the nature of liberation for gays and will attempt, eventually, to indicate directions." During the year there were many meetings, proposed re-organisations and actions, but none could stem the decline.[41]

One plan for revival called for a national Gay Pride week in September 1973. Coinciding with Pride week in the US, it was to be an extravaganza of events culminating in a march. "We want to bring the idea of Gay Liberation, first of all, before as many gays as possible, and second, confront the whole of society with our oppression and our demand for liberation."[42]

In contrast to the more separatist politics of later years Gay Lib welcomed solidarity from heterosexuals at the Gay Pride events. "It is also going to involve those heterosexuals who identify with the gay movement against the oppression of homosexuals – that's important as it is too easy to view all heterosexuals as our oppressors when these are people who are questioning and changing their attitudes towards us."[43]

One of the more notable, if gruesome, stunts during the week was a protest against lobotomies administered as a cure for homosexuality. Demonstrators set up a stall displaying lambs' brains and a sign "Homosexual Brains – Twenty Cents" outside a brain surgeon's rooms in Macquarie Street, Sydney. Afterwards they went into the surgeon's rooms, threw the brains on the floor and ground them into the carpet.[44]

The week was a success around the country, with the marches attracting up to 200 people.[45] Cops swooped on protesters in Sydney who were marching under the banner "Gay is Angry, Gay is Proud!", bashing and then arresting eighteen of them.[46] According to Lance Gowland, "We were handing out leaflets and the police told us to move on and we linked arms and the police were trying to push us...and we sat down and started to shout, 'this is what happens when homosexuals come out of the closet'...We were gonna fight, I was so angry!"[47]

Gay Pride Week 1973 marked both the highpoint and the end of the first, exuberant, optimistic and revolutionary phase of Gay Liberation. A time when "we believed we were making a new revolution; a clearly social revolution in which masculinity, femininity and institutionalised heterosexuality would all disappear."[48]

THE TURN TO RADICAL FEMINISM

There had been gains from two years of gay activism. Support for law reform in the polls had risen to 52 percent and campaigns in defence of victimised students and workers put anti-discrimination firmly on the agenda for unions. Hundreds, if not thousands of gays had "come out", begun throwing off the shackles of oppression, and life for so many was never going to be the same. Nonetheless times were changing.

Women's and Gay Liberation arose in the US and Britain at the height of a world-wide revolt against capitalism. From about 1974-1975 that revolt was ebbing world-wide, the Vietnam War was almost over and the capitalist class was on the offensive.

In Australia Gay Liberation which had started its rise towards the end of the period of revolt, could not sustain its early level of activism as the political situation began to turn down. The election of the Labor Party to federal government in 1972 had encouraged the poli-tics of lobbying in the halls of power, rather than demonstrating on the streets, cooption rather than confrontation.

The contradictions within the movement were intensified bringing to a head its limitations.

The theoretical leadership was still coming from the US and England, where radical feminism now predominated. Identity politics and separatism meant that socialist politics of working class alliance and mass struggle was marginalised. Appeals across class lines, rather than solidarity with the working class became dominant. While the radical left organisations had an influence out of proportion to their numbers, their small size put significant limits on their ability to argue for – and win – the alternative case for a socialist politics. Moreover, on the left, including some in the Communist Party of Australia, there was a shift towards adopting the radical feminist analysis, accepting this anti-Marxist critique. The result was a contorted amalgam called "socialist feminism", where, as Heidi Hartmann argued in *The unhappy marriage of Marxism and Feminism*, Marxism's supposed shortcomings were "corrected" by the addition of the feminist analysis. But this

Radical Feminism, whether theoretically linked to socialism or not, was an anti-Marxist ideology.

The Radical Feminist analysis first appeared in the gay movement in December 1972, introduced, in fact, by CPA member Pam Stein. There was no mention of the power of the working class to change society, instead women were pitted against biology (Nature) and men. "Radical feminism is not just a revival of a serious political movement for social equality. It is the most important revolution in history. It aims to over-throw the most rigid class and caste system in existence...the class system based on sex and the archetypal male and female roles. It is a struggle to break free from the oppressive power structures set up by Nature and reinforced by man."[49]

A Radicalesbian Conference in Sorrento in July 1973, spelt out the more separatist logic of the analysis in the US manifesto, *Woman Identified Woman*. "We believe that leadership is destructive, power is sexist... we work through actions and demonstrations to raise the consciousness of others, of male power, of leaderless societies." The Manifesto made clear it was a separate, women-only society they were aiming for. "We want to establish our own alternative feminist culture...there's no point in conquering male culture when we can create our own."[50]

Another conference, Lesbian Liberation in Minto at the end of 1973 moved even further rightwards, into a mythical past, discussing "lesbian martyres", "witches – our sisters", "covens – the future". Men were clearly *the* enemy and the future was a cross-class sisterhood, sharing the feelings and ideas "common to all lesbians, as well as common to all women".[51] Melbourne Gay Women's Group, around 60 members, ran small C-R sessions and had an action group where "we write leaflets and articles and plan protest action" about pornography, beauty contests and sexist advertising.[52]

Amongst some gay men, these radical feminist politics were expressed in the politics of Effeminism, a short-lived experiment mostly involving socialists. Published in May 1974 in the Monash University student paper *Lots Wife*, the Effeminist Manifesto spelt out what they stood for, in details reminiscent of the Radicalesbian Manifesto. They argued that "the oppression of women is basic to all other oppression."

Further men had to work to become "unmanly", to oppose hierarchies, to share, to be sensitive to the feelings of others, to raise children – in short, to live out what they claimed were alternative, non-masculine values.

Craig Johnston initially supported Effeminism. By mid 1975, however, he had recognised it to be a "defective analysis...the politics of individual guilt are not aids to revolutionary struggle...what the effeminists attempt is personal solutions which ignore the realities of actual power structures..." Nonetheless he still gave ground to the main thesis of radical feminism by emphasising how important it was "to insist on the primacy of the woman question and to relate the feminist analysis to our own lives", rather than arguing for the primacy of class.[53]

The adoption of radical feminist/radical lesbian politics was not the cause of the fragmentation. Radical feminism was a political choice by the majority of Gay and Women's Liberationists in response to the change in the political situation world-wide.

CHAPTER 5

GAY LIBERATION.
THE ROAD TO MARDI GRAS

1975 saw a revitalisation of the movement. It started in the Australian Union of Students, when a group of lesbian and gay students kicked off a campaign around AUS endorsed anti-discrimination motions. It was followed by a series of national conferences, the first of which attracted over six hundred. Over this period lesbian and gay workers won significant trade union support. This second phase ended on a high point in 1978 with the first Sydney Mardi Gras.

At the end of 1973 and without a clear political direction, Gay Lib had been in trouble. While the solutions that were proposed were organisational, the real problems were political. There were internal tensions – a failure to resolve the issue of sexism, the growing influence of radical feminist ideas that pulled women into women-only activism and organisations, away from joint work. And also a political failure to mesh the campaigns for reform with the need to build politically for revolutionary change, the need to build the political parties that could cohere the forces necessary to win. As socialist Angelo Rosas wrote in his assessment of Sydney Gay Liberation, "The key question, naturally enough was that of what revolution was to be achieved and as a result, what constituted revolutionary behaviour and action."[1]

Perhaps typical of discussions around the country was the February 1974 meeting of Sydney Gay Liberation. Rosas wrote that the meeting was "a forum for heated discussion, brought about, it seems, by the frustration of inaction". But no solutions emerged. Gay Pride Week in 1973, although a success in itself, failed to re-ignite Gay Lib. Two CPA members, Craig Johnston and Brian McGahen attempted to provide answers in their document, "Draft Statement of the Revolutionary Homosexuals on the Gay Liberation Front". Beginning, "Revolutionaries have fundamental objections to the present politics of the Sydney Gay Liberation Front", they listed the criticisms under three headings – Sydney GLF is individualistic, Sydney GLF is sexist, Sydney GLF is reformist.[2]

Johnston and McGahen outlined a program for action, whilst insisting theoretical issues had to be addressed. "Gay Liberation has to start working out a theory, covering women's oppression and its relation to homosexual oppression and has to put this into practice through a program which clearly expresses why Gay Liberation exists."

A year later another CPA member, Lance Gowland, wrote a more hard-hitting critique. Describing GLM as being "in the doldrums", he particularly attacked the movement for not supporting those who had supported them. "Mundey and Owens had the BLF unreservedly supporting our movement – we thank them by practically no support at any of their demonstrations."

He thought gays needed to learn from the mistakes of other struggles. The British homosexual law reform campaign had stopped before winning its main aims, and in fact the situation had gone backwards with more gays arrested than before the legal changes. "We should raise our demands above law reform and confront the causes of our oppression – eg, sexism and the economic structure. It should be explained to our gay sisters and brothers that there is no easy or quiet method of liberation...To bring about liberation we must work in organisations that are, or could be, allied to the homosexual cause... Gay brothers and sisters get off the fence!"[3]

Of course political activism did not disappear. As long as discrimination exists – as the 1980s AIDS and current gay marriage campaigns show – there will continue to be outbursts of protest. And this was definitely the case after 1973. There were some important campaigns during 1974-5 supporting teacher unionists. Gays joined the campaigns, rallies and demos over issues such as the coup in Chile and there was support for Indigenous causes with reciprocal backing. Gary Foley, then publicity officer for the Aboriginal Medical Service wrote to CAMP in 1975, noting that "We, as an oppressed minority group would like to express our solidarity with your group in our mutual struggle for recognition and fundamental freedom".[4]

1975 – revival on the campuses

The next *sustained* round of activism came from the campuses. During 1973 and 1974 a new layer of fighters was emerging at some of the universities. They began playing a role in the national student union – Australian Union of Students (AUS) – and from 1975 reignited lesbian and gay politics on the campuses and more broadly.

At the beginning of 1975 AUS Council met to determine its political direction. Phil Carswell recalls there was a "coalescence of talent and experience and capacity in one...critical mass", which had "an amazing impact".[5] Left wing students, close to or in the CPA, the Trotskyist groups and some independent leftists, were part of this critical mass.

Laurie Bebbington, a delegate from Melbourne University and Women's Officer for AUS, had already outlined some proposals to the campus Gay Lib group. At the beginning of the AUS Council she called a meeting – the Homosexual Caucus – to discuss pro-gay, anti-discrimination motions.[6]

Zap! an *occasional leaflet from the Homosexual Caucus*, listed nine motions to be put to the Council.[7] The most important pledged AUS to oppose all forms of discrimination, pushed for unbiased teaching in schools and called for the repeal of all anti-homosexual laws. Rather unexpectedly the motions were carried overwhelmingly. The Homosexual Caucus then pushed the issue further, calling for a Constituent Ratification process to take the motions to each campus. It was risky as earlier pro-Palestinian motions had been voted down in a CR process by students. But it was this move that politicised the campuses and encouraged the revival of activism.[8]

It created an issue that left wing groups and students could mobilise around. The International Socialist-aligned Revolutionary Communist club at Monash leafleted and carried articles in their newsletter *Hard Lines*. They argued that the cases of Penny Short and Jeremy Fisher proved that "AUS involvement in the Gay Rights issue is vital to defend a vulnerable minority of its members". The motions should be supported for being pro-gay rights, but also to "fight the sexual repressives of the church and rightwingers". The Communist Club made a more theoretical argument, about the role of the family and the capitalist system more generally. Some on the left were more critical of the motions. The SWP thought them ineffectual. Nonetheless they were "a welcome demonstration of solidarity with our fight".[9]

The campaign generated fierce debate. At Rusden College Phil Carswell remembers Christians coming across from Monash to heckle. At Monash there was opposition from the Christian right, future Liberal politician Peter Costello as well as the Maoists. Backing the AUS motion were the Women's and Gay Liberation groups and other left clubs. At LaTrobe the Maoists moved a countermotion to AUS's which opposed persecution of gays, while arguing Gay Lib was a product of US imperialism and a distraction from the struggle. Around the country, with some exceptions, the motions were voted up by a majority of the students.[10]

The motions promised more from AUS than sentiment. While Penny Short and Jeremy Fisher had received local campus student union support in 1973, the national AUS took no action. Movers of the motions in 1975 promised any future campaigns would get full AUS backing – and they delivered, as the Greg Weir case in 1977 was to show. Over several years AUS also funded a variety of surveys, publications and events, all aimed at keeping alive the issue of homosexual rights.

One of the most important initiatives was for AUS to underwrite and run a National Homosexual Conference. The first one, planned for August 1975, would be a new start for the movement as well as a uniting force for gay liberation.

Over 600 lesbians and gay men turned up to the first conference, to discuss everything from women's oppression to art and theatre. The atmosphere was electric, few had seen so many open homosexuals together in the one place. Papers for the sessions were listed under four main headings "Why homosexuals are oppressed", "How homosexuals are oppressed", "Homosexuals and feminism" and "Homosexual movements past and future". One of the most important initiatives at the conference was the formation of a Gay Teachers and Students Group, the first of the gay trade union support groups to appear.[11]

The organising collective's statement painted the conference as something new and separate from the earlier Gay Liberation events. It was also highly critical of Gay Lib, accusing it of a "moralistic, dogmatic ideology" irrelevant to the needs of most gays. This conference they insisted was not a GLM conference, it was aimed at the whole gay community, hence the workshops and papers on religion, lesbian mothers, gays and their families. However, the radical nature of the conference is clear from the main areas of discussion and the inclusion of a range of topics, including the issue of sexism, that were part and parcel of the radical agenda. After all male homosexuality was still illegal in most of the country and lesbian mothers lost custody of their children just for being gay. All the issues facing the community were seen as political and challenging to society.

The organised left were involved from the beginning, having been part of the AUS Homosexual Caucus and active on the campuses since the beginning of Gay Liberation. Several speakers from the CPA and the Trotskyist SWP spoke over the weekend, with the SWP's Richard Wilson and Ken Davis putting the case for an explicitly Marxist analysis of homosexual oppression and a working class-led revolution.

Ken Davis argued that, "We are not oppressed simply because we are different. Our oppression finds its foundations in the most basic institution of this society, the family. It is dependent on the class system and the subjugation of women. The overthrow of capitalism is the pre-condition for our liberation. Only after a socialist revolution can we destroy completely the economic and ideological foundations of the family." The way to build for revolution, Richard Wilson said, was for unity between lesbians and gay men. He added that "a collective oppression always necessitates a collective liberation".[12]

Feminism and Socialism – the debates

Sexism, however, continued to divide the movement. Laurie Bebbington and Marg Lyons delivered a stinging attack in their paper: "Why *should* we work with you? Lesbian-feminists versus 'gay' men". Arguing that the history of the gay struggle had been lesbians fighting both "with you and against you", they suggested that unity might never be possible as male homosexuals formed part of the patriarchal culture. "The fact that we are here has not made the differences between lesbians and male homosexuals disappear. Any number of utopian statements exhorting unity between homosexual women and men will not smooth over those differences. We regard our presence here as an uneasy and temporary coalition."

The relation between homosexuality and feminism, Bebbington and Lyons insisted, was *the* most important issue of the conference. "Feminism provides homosexuals with an analysis of society which has great explanatory power concerning homosexual oppression. It provides necessary directions for the liberation of ourselves as homosexual people."[13]

Three papers by male homosexuals also attempted to address these issues. "Effeminism", "Campfires of the resistance" and "Against a masculine society". All the authors were socialists, who argued the demands of gay liberation must incorporate a feminist/anti-sexist analysis. While the case for working together was made, there was also the proposition that men should consider organising separately, that there was no basis for a combined homosexual movement because of men's role in patriarchy, because of women and men's "separate oppression".[14]

Despite many papers and conferences; and joint and separate campaigns, this issue never went away. Sexism of course could not just 'go away', but the response to sexism itself and the radical feminist analysis that sought to deal with it in the gay movement were the critical issues. The practical result of acting on the feminist analysis was to propose withdrawing from joint work – both by women *and* men – a consequence that the left mainly, though not always, argued against. To work together or not continued to be a major issue, coming to a head in the lead up to the 1979 National Lesbian and Male Homosexual Conference in Melbourne. Following up a motion from 1978 which had proposed a separate event for lesbians because the movement's "sexism [was] so bad", meetings of the Melbourne Lesbian Action Group voted for a separate forum coinciding with the Fifth National Conference. Not all lesbians withdrew from joint work as the 1978 Mardi Gras events in particular were to show, but it did mark a weakening of forces.[15]

Despite the divisions and debates, the AUS-funded National Conferences, eleven in total, did become major rallying points for left wing forces. For socialist homosexuals these forums highlighted the need for some sort of broad left formation that could bring socialists together and to maximise the influence of socialist ideas. Just before the Second National Conference in August 1976 a group of gays mostly in the CPA put out a manifesto, aiming to provide the theoretical basis for left-wing gays to organise around.

The Manifesto of the Socialist Homosexuals outlined the role of the capitalist family in gay oppression, why sexism and the WLM mattered and why socialism was the solution. The *Manifesto* discussed the early gay rights movements and the gains of the Russian Revolution of 1917. It also took a stand against Stalinism and the parlous state of gays in China and Cuba, where "the revolutions that took place under the influence of world Stalinism...tended to reflect the Stalinist position on the homosexual question."[16]

The *Manifesto* also emphasised the need for unity between lesbians and gay men. Gay Liberation had started out as a mixed movement but had, the writers of the *Manifesto* commented, become confused in its politics. "Lesbians and male homosexuals began feeling united" but splits had occurred because of sexism.

Unity between lesbians and gay men was possible, but needed to go "hand-in-hand with the general struggle against sexism".

Five perspectives were outlined: to promote the organised defence of democratic rights for lesbians and male homosexuals; anti-sexism; the theoretical understanding of homosexual oppression; work in the trade unions, especially through homosexual caucuses and work amongst rank-and-file workers; and international solidarity.

The *Manifesto* argued the case for common interests between the working class and homosexuals. Socialism could only come through a revolutionary seizure of state power by the organised working class (and its allies), the only class with the potential to lead a revolution because of its size, organisation and base at the point of production. Not only did this involve unity and revolutionary consciousness, organisation and leadership in the working class, but also the forging of alliances with other classes and strata. Since both the working class and homosexuals had a common interest in the abolition of capitalism, there was ground for a principled alliance. Likewise with women and blacks: "Solidarity with each other's struggles today provides the basis for tomorrow's unity on the barricades."

In Sydney the Socialist Homosexuals met regularly for over a year, putting out a newsletter *Red and Lavender*. During 1977 the "What's On" section announced international solidarity demos for East Timor, at Qantas over striking Fijian workers and in protest over repression at Sharpeville in South Africa. Local campaigns included anti-Festival of Light, Movement against Uranium Mining, International Women's Day; as well there was the Marxism and Feminism Conference and a dance for Land Rights.

They debated the need for a political party, along with what was wrong with the ALP, as well as holding national conferences in 1977 and 1981. Two Sydney forums were held on "Can women and men work together as socialists?" and "Is there liberation through NSW parliament?" The question of reform versus revolution had been a constant in gay politics, with questions such as law reform for gay men and the involvement of CAMP in various government hearings into discrimination. Speakers at the forum "Is there liberation through NSW parliament" emphasised that seeking change through electoral means was fraught with problems. For socialists it was the class struggle between capitalists and workers that changed society. Building a political party that could "carry the class struggle through to the point of real change – the transition to socialism", was the goal.[17]

Union solidarity

Workers and their trade unions were believed to be indifferent or even hostile to lesbians and homosexuals. Often this belief turned out to be wrong. In fact amongst the first organisations to take action in support of victimised gays were the blue-collar Builders Labourers Federation and the white-collar NSW Teachers Federation.[18]

In December 1972, the current affairs program Dateline ran a one hour special on homosexuality. They interviewed two young men, both called Alan, a tram driver and a storeman, both of whom had been threatened with eviction by their landlord if they appeared on TV. As part of the program the film crew did street interviews and went into a local pub frequented by waterside workers. Their street survey found only two people "antagonistic towards homosexuals" and none of the wharf labourers "was outrightly opposed to homosexuals". The channel itself got more than 100 congratulatory phone calls.[19]

The trade union response to discrimination against gays was actually quicker and more substantial than from government or employers. From the first reported case of discrimination in 1974, writes Shane Ostenfeld, it took only two years for a generalised anti-discrimination policy to be adopted by the peak union councils, CAGEO, ACSPA and the ACTU. Within four years ACSPA and CAGEO had specific lesbian and gay anti-discrimination policies in place, while the ACTU adopted similar policies after its amalgamation with the other two bodies. ACSPA, in 1979, also hosted a joint meeting of gay unionists, blue and white collar. The cross-membership between students, the women's and lesbian and gay movements and the revolutionary parties, adds Ostenfeld, "provided the network necessary for the adoption of progressive policies in left-leaning unions of the blue collar and white collar working class". It was also an area of work where lesbians and male homosexuals could unite.[20]

Gay organisations recognised the problem of discrimination, from workplace bullying to sackings. Early on *Camp Ink* ran a piece on "Coming Out at Work". Starting with "One of the best experiences of my life has been coming out at work", the article emphasised that it wasn't just because it made the writer feel better. It was something of "special importance to gays in the movement, because this is where Gay Power lies, in the working class".[21]

The left continually pushed the movement towards the working class, seeking support from the trade unions, arguing the case for solidarity. Seeing the need for mass struggle, the Socialist Homosexuals argued that "The more we fight, the more of us who fight, the harder it will be for the system to oppress individuals."[22] The campaigns were part of a broader struggle. The Greg Weir campaign (see below), as *Red and Lavender* explained in September 1977, was more than a campaign about employment or compensation, it was a challenge to oppression and part of the fight against capitalism.

At the Second National Homosexual Conference in 1976, both the Socialist Homosexual and the Job Discrimination workshops urged lesbians and gay men to be active in their unions, and form caucuses within them. They called for the ACTU to develop its own anti-discrimination policy. The opening plenary was "Education and the Homosexual" and five of the 33 workshops during the weekend were on trade unions or job discrimination.

The education system was a target of homosexual activists because teachers were particularly vulnerable to employment discrimination, and because sex education for students was such a 'hot-button' topic for right wing groups and newspaper editorials.

In the early days of Gay Liberation when speakers were visiting schools to talk to students, the *Age* had railed that "Gay Lib is a cultist deviation with a tendency to seek recruits wherever it can find them, particularly among adolescents. Members of the cult have few qualifications as lecturers to students."[23]

The Third Conference featured a major plenary session on gays and the workforce. It held workshops on the Greg Weir campaign and a plan to introduce an agenda item on anti-discrimination at the 1979 ACTU congress. Socialists put a motion to the final plenary that the Fourth Conference be on Lesbians and Male Homosexuals in the Workforce, or Homosexuals at Work as it became known.[24] One outcome was the Gay Trade Unionists Group because, as Laurie Bebbington summed up, "this is where the strength lies".[25]

Union sentiment was growing. When the Plumbers Union adopted new policy, it said that "Homosexual discrimination is an industrial issue and has to be fought on that basis". The union would seek to remove discriminatory provisions in awards, including issues such as bereavement leave. For John Rutherford, PGEU Assistant General Secretary and CPA member, "The fact that the motion was endorsed without amendment and with minimal objection is evidence of the Union's concern for all of the membership."[26]

But governments continued to blatantly discriminate. Ministers for Education in both Queensland and NSW made it clear openly gay teachers of either sex would not be employed. This meant that teachers were amongst the first to raise and fight for anti-discrimination policies covering women, migrants and then gays in their unions. The teacher unions, by and large, were sympathetic. The Communist-led NSWTF had long experience, dating from the late 1950s of police harassing gay male teachers. In one case, it seems, the police were reluctant to charge someone they'd apprehended on a beat when they realised he was an activist with the teachers union.[27]

In June 1976 two hundred came to a union-sponsored seminar of gay teachers. Here they discussed the cases of Penny Short and

Mike Clohesy, a teacher who'd been sacked from a Sydney Catholic School; and a media-run campaign in Melbourne opposing gay speakers visiting schools. The Victorian Secondary Teachers Association AGM that year adopted an "abolition of sexism" motion, which laid the basis for its Open Committee on Homosexuality. Phil Carswell pays tribute to John Lewis, the convenor, saying that while "individuals are not the motor of history, class is, but individuals can be catalysts and that's what John was".

The next major campaign was for student teacher Greg Weir. As a student at Brisbane's Kelvin Grove Teachers College in 1976, Weir had led a successful campaign to have the campus gay club recognised. For this, Education Minister Val Bird publicly announced that Weir, though bound through his scholarship to teach in Queensland, would never teach in a government school.

Gays immediately set up a campaign group in Queensland and at the 1977 AUS Council there was a motion launching a national campaign around rights for homosexuals at work and as students. While the focus of the campaign was funding for a Breach of Contract legal case, Weir called on gays to get their unions to support him and pressure Education Ministers around the country to publicly agree not to discriminate.[28]

"It's too much of a hot potato", was the shameful commentary from the Queensland Teachers' Federation. The union explained it had been wrong-footed in the 1976 case of a teacher disciplined over marihuana use, adding that because Greg wasn't actually teaching he couldn't be a member of the QTF. However the union did make representations to the Education Department, getting back a swathe of contradictory reasons – never his homosexuality – why it had refused Weir employment. As late as 1984 Queensland Education Minister Lin Powell declared that teachers in State schools who publicaly declared they were homosexual would be sacked immediately.[29]

Though he finally won a court settlement in 1983, Greg never taught in Queensland. An attempt to teach in NSW was also stymied when the Education Minister there took his name off the teacher register because of Weir's "expressed attitudes in relation to homosexuality". It did fire up the campaign in NSW, but the Wran Labor government proved more susceptible to pressure from the Churches and other right-wing forces.

Nonetheless the breadth of the campaign, which AUS promoted around the country, with national rallies, sessions at the National Homosexual Conferences, local campaign groups and newsletters was path-breaking, the first such campaign run by AUS.[30] While going to the courts is often problematic, the law being there to uphold the system rather than challenge it, it was only one part of the campaign. It was the nationwide implications of the case that were important. An early campaign report noted: "We must not dismiss Greg's case as being a product of [Premier] Joh Bjelke-Petersen or Queensland. Greg's case is a litmus test... for Australian lesbians and male homosexuals – and for the rights and welfare of trainee teacher students and all students throughout Australia." Campaigns such as this ensured unions fought back more effectively and more gays were prepared to be open.[31]

Gays, as workers, had to take the lead in their unions too. Representatives from a range of unions, one report noted, "hammered the same point – unions will not adopt anti-discrimination policies to protect gay members unless the initiative comes from grass-roots level and has widespread support."[32] By the end of the 70s there was a growing list of unions which supported or adopted anti-discrimination policies, some of whom had taken action to back their members.[33] Melbourne University cafeteria workers set an example by their in-principle support for a student evicted from Graduate House residential college. Terry Stokes had been part of a protest over the earlier arrest of two young men for kissing in public, in Collins Street outside a gay venue. Gays organised a "kiss-in" some days later and Terry and his "kiss-in partner" were arrested for offensive behaviour. Twenty students occupied Graduate House for four hours and the warden promised an appeal would be heard. In the meantime Terry was evicted.

Six days later came the union action. Reported in *The Gay Trade Unionist:* "On the 16 October, the workers at the University Union Caf stopped work. The Liquor Trades Union shop steward moved a motion condemning 'the eviction for what is claimed as homosexual behaviour'. In support of the motion she said that the Victorian laws unjustly discriminated against homosexuals. She added that if Terry's appeal was not upheld, further stop-work meetings would be held and other unions contacted." On October 18 the Board decided to re-admit him.[34]

A significant development between 1976 and 1979 was the incorporation of anti-discrimination clauses by the peak union bodies. These policy moves were critical in getting changes to the award system which controlled the standard conditions and wages on the job. Adoption of progressive policies, as Ostenfeld notes, also created pressure for wider change and increased the pressure on the Labor Party. Later, these union and ALP links were to prove invaluable in the campaigns around HIV-AIDS and in teaching.[35]

1975 had re-energised and re-mobilised gays to fight for their rights. There had been significant gains since then for students on campus, for workers through their unions and many were confident of future improvements. While 1976 and 1977 kept the momentum going, it was 1978 that was the highlight, its impact on a par with the arrival of Gay Liberation. On the positive side, there were important breakthroughs such as the first pro-gay resource book for school kids, *Young, Gay and Proud* and the adoption of an anti-discrimination policy by the country's biggest employer, the federal public service. Gays and supporters marched on May Day in Melbourne with banners such as "The gay 10% is everywhere – unions must support their homosexual members".[36]

But darker forces were also at work.

From the mid-1970s the Right was on the attack. The Whitlam government had been sacked in 1975 and replaced by a right-wing Liberal government determined to defeat workers' organisations and undo many welfare and social benefits. There was widespread talk of a backlash against the gains won by gays and women and in the context of the ongoing attacks overseas and against workers in Australia, this was a legitimate concern.

Overseas, especially in the English-speaking world rights were under attack. 1977 had seen pro-gay statutes overturned in the US, in Canada *Body Politic* was facing charges in the courts. Morals campaigner Mary Whitehouse had been successful in prosecuting *Gay News*, the leading magazine in Britain. The US and British defeats were the first real failures of lesbian and gay campaigns since Stonewall.

In Australia the Festival of Light (FoL), a conservative Christian group, arranged for Whitehouse to tour during 1978. The tour, however, ended up a flop after demonstrations met her every appearance. Gay workers' rights were under attack too when the Joh Bjelke-Petersen government in Queensland banned Greg Weir from teaching. In NSW there was a marked increase in police harassment around the bars, including lesbian bars and the beats, possibly part of a police dispute with the Wran ALP government to increase powers. At the same time homosexual law reform had stalled. Only in South Australia and the ACT was gay male sex semi-legal, anywhere else you could still be jailed. In NSW lesbians and gay men were incensed that Premier Neville Wran had reneged on promised law reform, bowing to pressure from the religious right.

Mardi Gras...It was a riot!

In Canada *Body Politic* eventually won its case and in the US gays were campaigning, holding back some of the Right's attacks with community and union-based campaigns. Warning against letting anti-homosexual groups grow, gay groups in Sydney called for a mobilization against Mary Whitehouse's tour. By January 1978 the Social Freedom Action Coalition (later anti-FoL), was set up, mobilizing similar groups in the cities Whitehouse was planning to visit.[37]

In one of the biggest shows of strength since the Right's offensive in the US, San Francisco's gay community mobilised 375,000 at the June 1977 Gay Pride Day Parade, then issued a call to the international lesbian and gay community for solidarity action the following year.

SWP members Ken Davis and Annie Taylor responded to the call and organised a meeting for May 20 to form a Gay Solidarity Group. The GSG planned a demonstration then by a public meeting. CAMP executive member Ron Austin and Lance Gowland proposed further action, a night-time celebration or Mardi Gras. GSG backed the Mardi Gras proposal, with a caveat, Austin and Gowland would have to do the organizing as everyone else was too busy.

The response to every event on the day was beyond anyone's expectations. It was fuelled by a frustration suggests Ken Davis, "that although the movements in other countries, notably the United States, were making advances and fighting, not much was happening here".[38]

To begin the day, 500-strong, lesbians and gay men marched through the city, banners held high, demanding the repeal of homophobic laws and solidarity with struggles around the world. Then it was off to a public meeting on gay rights and finally the Mardi Gras.

It was well into the night of June 24, 1978 and Sydney's gays were determined to finish off a day of political action with the Mardi Gras. "Sing if you're glad to be gay" and "Ode to a gym teacher" belted out as the parade made its way down Oxford Street, Sydney's "gay mile". Building the numbers along the way, close to 2000 people sang and chanted "out of the bars and into the streets, join us" as they headed for Hyde Park.

The trouble started at the Park. Low level harassment at first, with the cops hassling Lance Gowland, the driver of the lead truck, as he read out messages of support. When he wouldn't stop, they pulled him out of the truck, then confiscated it and the PA system. Angrier, arms linked, the parade headed for Kings Cross, all the time with the police pushing and closing off streets.

On reaching the El Alamein fountain, the mood was uglier. Unsure what would happen, the crowd started turning to go back along the parade route. And as they did suddenly the divvy vans appeared, police pouring out and laying into the crowd, kicking, punching and bundling people into the vans. The demonstrators fought back. 53 were arrested. One lesbian vividly recalls "I was just wild, ecstatic and screaming up and down the street, 'Up the lezzos!' I did get arrested for saying that."

Joseph Chetcuti, one of the Mardi Gras revellers, recalls: "We had had enough of the state and the church telling us what to do with our bodies...a crowd of mostly gay men and lesbians stood up to the police. The Stonewall riots may well have been a watershed for the worldwide gay and lesbian rights movement but for Australia, the Mardi Gras of 1978 was our first very public act of resistance and a turning point in our struggle against oppression."

On Monday morning demonstrators gathered again as the 53 were brought before the courts. With the cops barricading the entrances few could get in, and as scuffles broke out another seven were arrested. "The police were trying to break our spirit." They failed. Instead as one lesbian explained "I felt I belonged to something and I was going somewhere...I was beginning to get an understanding of what politics and power were all about."

There were solidarity demonstrations in other major cities and in Sydney 300 met on July 1 to organise the next protest. Two weeks after Mardi Gras 2000 demonstrators retraced the June 24 route, carrying banners such as "Lesbians Ignite!" Hundreds had been mobilised for the day including some from the trade unions and ALP branches. As the march, the biggest gay demonstration Australia had ever seen, reached the police station there was a clash and 13 more were arrested. Six weeks later, Sydney hosted the Fourth National Homosexual Conference. Again lesbians and gays decided to march, this time with the added goal of confronting the anti-abortion Right to Life who were rallying in the city. The police made mass arrests again, adding to the sense of public outrage, further fuelling the "Drop the Charges" campaign.

By the end of 1979 the police had quietly dropped the charges, claiming they'd lost the files. The actions had won the "right to march" for everyone. The campaign had forced the NSW government to repeal the hated Summary Offences Act, the law police had used to try to stop earlier protests by gays and a wide range of other groups. As Ken Davis emphasises, "It was the single most important law reform for lots of us - gay, straight, Indigenous."

Buoyed by this success and the boost from other activities during the year, lesbians and gays decided to launch a Summer Offensive for the beginning of 1980, as well as a Campaign Against Repression against the upcoming International Year of the Child, a year that was being hijacked by conservative forces.

But by the end of the 1970s Gay Liberation was no longer, its limits had been reached. Revolution was no longer 'in the air' and the focus was on reform and providing welfare and legal services for a lesbian and gay clientele. "The gay movement of the seventies is now the gay community of the eighties", Terry Goulden wrote in *klick!*. He believed it was a step forward, bringing "the broadest possible unity and political credibility".[39]

However going from "movement" to "community" was, in reality a move away from revolutionary politics to those of working within the system, spearheaded by Communist Party activists who were replicating what the party was doing elsewhere.[40] Craig Johnston, one of the prime movers and chroniclers of the shift, laid this out explicitly in a paper to the Socialism and Homosexuality Conference in 1981. "This is the role for gay radicals: help in the unifications/solidification of the gay subcultures, help them to explore their way politically and to develop clout. That is, build a gay community." He summarised the process as changing the political framework from "Oppression to Discrimination, from Liberation to Rights and from Movement to Community".[41]

The turn to community politics, including the re-badging of Mardi Gras as a festival rather than a protest, rather than signalling a rebirth of Gay Liberation, marked the end of "liberation" politics. One of the badges from 1978 declared: "Mardi Gras was a riot – now we need a revolution!" The early

Gay Liberation had promised revolution, but by 1978 the 60s revolutionary fervour had passed and there was a worldwide downturn in political and industrial activity. The revolution had been postponed.

None of this can take away from the gains of Gay Liberation. It was transformational. It changed lives, millions of people's lives worldwide, with its defiance and pride. In Australia, as elsewhere, the movement – and the activists that built it – made it possible for people to live, work and love more freely. Discrimination and oppression still existed, but Gay Lib gave lesbians and gays more strength to continue the fight against discrimination and laid the basis for campaigns to come.

CHAPTER 6

RED AND LAVENDER

"Gay Liberation has a perspective for revolution based on the *unity of all oppressed people*. There can be no freedom for gays in a society that enslaves others through male supremacy, racism and economic exploitation (capitalism)."[1] These were the words of the GLF's first leaflet in 1972. It's no surprise then that the demands of Gay Liberation would mesh with those of the radical left, the newly formed Trotskyist groups and the evolving CPA, as well as some in the left unions.

Working class? Middle class? The new liberation movements

Rather than the left and the working class, however, it is commonly asserted that it was a new liberal current, a new middle class — students, intelligentsia and professionals — that fuelled the rise of movements such as GL. This is the thesis of Graham Willett's major history of the Australian gay movement, *Living Out Loud*.[2] Craig Johnston also proposed such an analysis at the end of 1978: "In the imperialist heartlands sections of the young petty bourgeoisie broke with the dominant ideologies and attempted to revitalise traditional liberal precepts with their own *jacquerie* [peasant revolt]. Successive waves of protest flowed and ebbed — anti-war, student, blacks, women, homosexuals."[3]

While there's no doubt a radicalising layer of this new middle class played an important role, particularly on the campuses, that is only a partial picture of this turbulent period. It overlooks the fact that this was a time when tertiary education opened up for workers and many a lecturer found most of their students were working class and more class conscious than they expected.[4] The role of intellectuals is also misinterpreted as Verity Burgmann points out: "Intellectuals do not, in the main, invent liberating ideas and impose them on people who then form social movements; rather intellectually trained people are important in articulating and embellishing ideas that are being worked out in practice, in and by the movements themselves..." More importantly, ascribing the leading role in the radicalisation to a new middle class can only seem true if you view it out of context, ignoring the mass working class mobilisations of the time or the links between the social movements and the working class.[5]

Far from depending on a new middle class, the strongest social movements always had connections with the labour movement. The point was clearly illustrated at a 2001 conference, *The Turbulent Decade*, documenting activism in the years 1965-1975 in Australia. One after another, activists in social movements as diverse as anti-apartheid, anti-war, land rights, gays and women, all detailed links between trade unions, the left groups and their particular causes.[6]

Ken Davis told the conference how he had joined the Socialist Youth Alliance (SYA) as well as the local ALP branch in 1972 while he was still at school, and a year before he came out. Despite SWP/SYA support for gay liberation, Davis initially questioned why sexuality would be of interest to working class or left wing groups. It was Marxism that "taught me that...our sexual lives were socially constructed and it was not a question of personal blame." The BLF support for Jeremy Fisher and Penny Short was also important in changing Davis's view. Davis came out the day the left had organised a rally in support of the Allende government in Chile. It was also the day of Sydney's first Gay Pride demonstration. He went to both, commenting that "there was a tremendous intersection between a whole lot of issues, whether we liked it or not."[7]

Unions responded to the activists' calls for anti-discrimination policies or support in cases of victimisation. A telling comparison is how quickly the organised working class took up gay rights, as opposed to members of Parliament who dragged their feet, sometimes for decades, on homosexual law reform.

But overall, it was Marxism – and the left political organisations – which brought all those issues into a coherent world view and outlined a strategy for change; that linked the fight of all the oppressed with class struggle against the system of capitalism. The strength of the communist position, says Phil Carswell, was that it drew "this *absolute* connection between homosexuality and feminism and the fight for gay rights *and* the fight against capitalism... [that they were] inextricably linked...It gave people a chance to have a world view and an organised political response."[8]

In this radicalising period three different left groups – the CPA, the Socialist Workers Party and the International Socialists – were a significant part of the struggle on the shop floor and in the radical movements. The rest of the left played a different role. The pro-Beijing CPA(ML) or Maoists, who were influential on some campuses and unions, distinguished themselves by their Stalinist politics. Though they opposed the persecution of homosexuals, they actively opposed gay groups on campus, claiming Gay Liberation was a tool of US imperialism and a distraction from the struggle. The pro-Moscow Socialist Party of Australia (SPA) did not support gay rights, but was less actively hostile than the CPA(ML). While the Spartacist League formally supported the liberation movements, they only played a cameo, and not always welcome, role in the campaigns.[9]

This book concentrates on the role of those groups actively supporting Gay Liberation – the CPA, SWP and IS. The biggest of the three, the CPA was the first party to respond – even before a group had formed in Australia. As Denis Freney notes in his autobiography he'd been reading reports of the new movement in the Trotskyist papers from the US and "found the militancy and leftism of Gay Liberation in the USA much more to my liking (than the more reformist CAMP)."[10] *Tribune* [26 May 1971] carried the first serious article in the Australian press, left or otherwise on Gay Liberation – by Freney.

The Communist Party of Australia

The CPA's early history had seen it championing sexual freedom. This was followed by Stalinist reaction. However the party was still more progressive than much of society, challenging censorship, fighting for women's rights especially in the areas of birth control and wages as well as reviewing plays, books and even poetry which challenged depictions of society and personal relationships. A number of the Communist Party members were noted – and notorious – authors and playwrights, performing in radical theatre and joining in the literary debates of the day. Peter Murphy, a party member from the 1970s, notes that much of the literature that the Party defended in their anti-censorship and free speech campaigns was banned on the grounds of obscenity because of its sexual content.[11]

Nonetheless it wasn't till the mid 1960s that homosexuality was more positively portrayed in the CPA press. Some Party members were expelled or denied membership when their homosexuality was discovered, and some others lived in fear of discovery. One analysis paints a negative and in my view incorrect analysis of the party's attittudes. In her thesis *Pinks under the bed*, Kate Davison concluded from her interviews with a number of CPA members that there was an "internal atmosphere of self-regulation and fear of surveillance" which was like that imposed by the state, leading to a heightened sense of scrutiny. She said that the party's approach, far from "challenging the construction of homosexuality as a threat to the nation...the criminality [of homosexuality] resulted in its transferral into a threat to the Party...as something foreign, untrustworthy...in many ways reinforcing and strengthening state regulation of sexuality."[12]

Despite the party's claim to an internationalist platform, Davison argues that where homosexuality was concerned, the CPA merely mirrored the state it opposed. She also says this stand was a "contributing factor to the delayed emergence of a resistance movement against homophobia in the late 1960s."[13]

Homosexuals actually had mixed experiences in the Party – from acceptance to expulsion – and the Party's record on censorship and other "social" issues tells a more nuanced story, not a simple mirroring of the state. Moreover, unlike the state which had a vested interest in maintaining homophobia, the CPA, despite the Stalinist distortions, had the political basis and early history to draw on, to enable it to recover its progressive tradition and support homosexual liberation. The CPA had no powers of repression comparable to those of the state.

For Peter Murphy the Stalinist period from the 1930s to 1960s was an aberration. He argues that "the left position overall is to support the rights of minorities, women's rights". And Davison herself warned against categorising the "failure of left-wing and progressive forces to challenge homophobia...as homophobia". It's worth noting here, too, that in a number of European countries – including some in the Eastern bloc – gay sex was not illegal. Nonetheless it cannot be denied that Stalinism played a part in holding back the fight for liberation in a large part of the world for many decades.[14]

To bring the party in Australia back to a more progressive stance would take three developments: first among homosexuals themselves, then changes in the political climate and finally within the CPA.

Firstly, as Teachers Union organiser and Labor Party member Bill Leslie described, it meant breaking through the framework that viewed homosexuality as a crime. Homosexuals themselves had to become "self aware", to know themselves as a group with shared interests. This self-awareness was essential before gays could recognise they had rights, could organise to fight for those rights. This was something that the homophile movement in the US had taken twenty years to develop. It happened within a few short months in Australia in early 1970.[15]

If, for example, Laurie Collinson had succeeded in establishing a homosexual law reform committee in 1958, it could have overcome some of the limitations Leslie refers to. After all, Australia was very similar to the UK in both laws and attitudes. CPA support for Collinson's attempt might also have meant success in forming a law reform group and we know not everyone in the party was hostile to homosexuality. However if we compare CPA response to two reform movements – homosexuality and abortion – party support may not have made much difference. The CPA consistently supported abortion law reform in spite of Russia criminalising it from the mid 1930s. However, a serious campaign around abortion didn't get underway in Australia until the arrival of the Women's Liberation Movement. It was the changed political environment that made a difference. It was then that the Communist Party (and others on the left) could seize the opportunity to set up and build the liberation movements and more effective campaigns for reform.

Radicalising times

The radicalisation of the late 60s led to the party recruiting a number of young students and workers, especially around the anti-Vietnam War movement. Some of these also joined Gay Liberation. It was these recruits – albeit supported by older members as we'll see – who pushed within the CPA for a policy change, for Communists to act against the oppression of lesbians and gay men. Both the influx of younger activists and the 60s radicalisation were essential features in altering policy in the CPA.

Finally, support for gays didn't come without other political developments inside the party. The CPA was in trouble as it entered the 1970s, smaller and more divided than it had been for decades, so it needed to cohere a new politics and grow if it was to survive. Critical to transforming the party's position on gays was its new political stance in relation to Stalinism, the USSR and the Eastern Bloc countries, as well as to students and the new liberation movements. The Party had split over these issues and though the fragmentation was disruptive it opened the CPA up to the wave of radicalisation and enabled it to grow again. Peter Murphy argues that the big split of 1968-71, ostensibly about the invasion of Czechoslovakia, was as much about the role of women and the emerging Women's Liberation Movement. In 1967 the party, he says, was already splitting over the question of women, "democracy at work" and the environment, experiencing a "huge, 'rough' fight" over women's demands at the 1967 Congress.

As well, underpinning everything was the ferment over the Vietnam War. "People had to be courageous", Murphy adds, "so it meant that grass roots members felt they were empowered and were less willing to accept the hierarchy of the party". Women too were energised by the anti-Vietnam war actions and started to make demands.

In the end it was not enough to save the Party, a reflection of the overall problems with its political trajectory. The CPA moved away from Stalinism, but not toward revolutionary Marxist politics; rather it drifted towards western social-democratic perspectives. This was an essentially conservative trend. However the party's conservative direction also intersected, after 1968, with a profound social radicalisation. It also created space for liberationist sexual politics to take root.[16]

Gay Liberation comes to the CPA

From the late 60s and into the 1970s, the CPA hoped it could regroup and survive.

A full page article on Gay Liberation, detailing the Bolsheviks' early progressive stance, had appeared in *Tribune* in mid 1971. Although Denis Freney said the article was well received, he knew some in the party would find it difficult to accept. But he was determined to see it in print. "I felt it was necessary to tackle such issues, not only because I was directly affected by the oppression of homosexuals, but because, if the CPA was to survive the trauma of de-stalinisation, its members would have to leave behind all aspects of Stalinist oppression."[17]

Numerous recollections point to significant backing within the CP for gay liberation, or at least rights for homosexuals. Many thank the women members who fought within the party, first over Women's Liberation and then Gay Liberation. Lesbians and gay men, according to Peter Murphy, could not have won without the likes of Joyce Stevens and Mavis Robertson and other sympathetic members.[18]

Phil Carswell describes a debate at a CPA National Congress, where a gay rights resolution was put up by Freney and other openly gay members. "I don't recall the debate being acrimonious or hostile, but I do remember a lot of well-meaning working class comrades really struggling with it, really finding it hard to say, 'why is this a revolutionary issue?'" But people "understood shared oppressions... There was a solidarity between people...it resonated with their experiences as either members of the working class or as women, or as Indigenous or migrant..." The gay rights resolution passed.

In fact Phil found that anti-Communism amongst lesbians and gay men outside the party was a far greater problem than homophobia within the CPA.

Some opposition remained. There were some sharp debates in the letters pages of *Tribune*, but less and less opposition as the coverage of gay issues increased. But, of course, homophobia couldn't just be waved away; while capitalism remained intact anti-gay sentiment would not disappear. It had to be continually opposed, whether in society at large or within the CPA. As late as 1978 Brian McGahen was to condemn lingering homophobia in the Party, manifested more by absence of homosexual issues in party policy statements, publications and forums, than by overt hostility.[19]

Consequently lesbians and gays in the party and their supporters kept the question before Party members through *Tribune* or other forums, as well as working in unions and party meetings. For example, Narelle Colman spoke at the 1973 NSW South Coast District Conference, with a Party forum "Marxism and Human Liberation" addressed by Craig Johnston in Newcastle later that year.[20] At the Wollongong forum, the mostly working class branch carried a six-point resolution, detailing support for lesbian and gay rights.[21]

Peter Murphy acknowledges the CPA wasn't always the first to raise gay issues, but says the party "rapidly recognised the importance of Gay Liberation and gave it quite a lot of impetus". In fact the Communist youth group had supported homosexual rights from 1971, while it took less than a year after Gay Liberation appeared for the party to change its public position.

From then on the Communist Party regularly covered the topic in *Tribune*. It did use the paper for some longer, more theoretical or historical articles, for example a survey of the situation for gays in the Soviet bloc and retrospectives on the gay movement. However most of the theoretical discussion appeared in internal congress documents or publicaly in the gay press. Among CPA members, Denis Freney, Craig Johnston, Lance Gowland and Brian McGahen played the most prominent role in the gay press.

The Communist Party adopted its first pro-gay resolution in 1972. Moved by Lance Gowland and Denis Freney, it read in part: "The CPA believes that the legal basis for police persecution and prosecution of homosexuals and social and economic discrimination against them must be ended and homosexuals accepted as full citizens..."[22] By 1973 Freney was putting a more radical line in public, talking about oppression, liberation and revolution. In *Tribune* during Gay Pride week he argued that oppression was systemic and just changing the law could not end it.[23]

At the party's 1974 Easter Congress a more substantial policy expressed the importance the CPA gave to winning the working class to fight against all oppression. The resolution rejected the notion of homosexuality as a disease, or a product of "decadent capitalism" that would be "cured" by socialism. Homosexuality was a "valid form of sexual expression". The links between the fight against homosexual oppression and women's oppression were emphasised.

The new policy made a strong statement for autonomous organising. It was argued that an independent movement was better placed to break down any anti-homosexual sentiments within the Communist Party and amongst workers. "The liberation of homosexuals must be largely the work of homosexuals themselves. The CPA, basing itself on the principle of self-determination for all oppressed groups and self-management does not tell homosexuals how to run their movement for their liberation. Communist homosexuals do, however, point out that in a society where anyone is oppressed, no one can be free and [communist homosexuals] view their struggle as militant homosexuals as part of the total, human, self-managed socialist revolution."[24]

The CPA was the biggest group on the left with organised forces in workplaces, in campaigns and on the campuses. With the changes in the late 60s and early 70s it was able to win new members and supporters around its position on gays. The party's members were well placed to intervene in the movement both theoretically and practically; in the unions around anti-discrimination legislation and more broadly for law reform. Party members were able to play a major role in the "Gays at Work" conference in 1978, for example, through the CPA's contacts in the union movement and ALP[25]

This didn't mean there were hundreds of lesbians and gay men in and around the party; the numbers of activists were in the tens, with women roughly half that number, scattered around the country. However as Peter Murphy argues relatively small numbers organised around a political position could have "an inordinate impact on the trajectory and broad social outcomes of a movement". It was because of gays working within the party winning policy changes, that CPA member and State Secretary of the NSW BLF Jack Mundey could encourage his union members to take action to protest the victimisation of gay students Jeremy Fisher and Penny Short. The NSW Teachers Federation, with CPA members in the union and the leadership, was likewise an ally. The teachers' unions were among the first to develop policies and action around women's and gay demands.

Within the party, as in WLM, homosexuals organised their work through committees, though these were usually only convened before major events. Rather than the leadership making decisive interventions and mobilising members, it was more a case of "let everything happen and we'll help it happen". Phil Carswell argues that "Once you had the basic principles of equity, struggle, a better world, collective action, respect for people, respect for their opinions, then everything else really flowed on…" It was the Gay Collective, for example, which organised visits to various industrial branches to discuss the question of sexual politics.

A Collective report gives a picture of CPA activities. They held a reading group to form a "principled Marxist position on sexuality" and contributed to a debate in *Tribune*. There was also a "Wednesday night at the CPA" series on sexuality. The Collective helped develop national congress policies and members were active in the Gay Trade Unionist Group, Young Gays and Gay Youth Accommodation. The report concluded that members were "increasingly influential in the gay community because of their principled position, ability and consistency of work".[26]

However although there was a general political position in the party, there was not always a particular "line", a fact for which they were sometimes roundly criticised by others. Phil Carswell defends this approach, explaining, "It wasn't like there was a doctrinaire response to an issue. It was 'okay, what's the most progressive thing we can do here, what's the thing that will get the best outcome for the most people?'" The party was criticised for what many saw as opportunism, but for Phil it was a matter of dealing with the fact that while you could never get full agreement, you could win people to change.[27]

Mardi Gras and the shift to the community

Questions about the way forward, how to win the best outcome are a constant within movements, often becoming more focussed and heated when campaigns reach a high point. 1978 represented just such a time and the CPA had already begun looking for new directions in its gay work. Although the party was committed to range of campaigns, Peter Murphy says: "We felt like we were doing the same thing over and over again, but getting nowhere, not even getting bigger...we had to do something new." Party members found themselves working more and more with the community sector on the rationale that, as Phil Carswell argued, "our politics said if you're going to create mass change, you got to go where the masses are". That meant going to the bars and the community, as well as workplaces in what the party saw as a more sustained level of commitment, alongside a reduced emphasis on activism "on the streets". It was even about having fun, Peter Murphy says.

Mardi Gras provided apparent vindication. Lance Gowland later recalled everyone's shock when the evening celebration attracted so many more than the morning's political march. They immediately concluded that "we had found a way of breaking through the barrier that exists between the political gays and the non-political gays and we were onto a really wonderful event".[28]

Here, it seemed was the confirmation some in the Communist Party were seeking for their plans to "shift to the community". For Lance it was also justification for the coalition politics he'd argued that the CPA believed in, the type of politics he claimed others opposed. "We believed in working with the green movements, the social movements", whereas for the other left groups, "the idea was to get massive strikes and things and bring down the capitalist society...[their] focus was only on the trade unions..."[29]

Not everyone supported a turn to the community, and the Gay Collective's proposed position for the party's 1979 program seemed to emphasise a more class-based approach. Craig Johnston wrote that they aimed to develop a Marxist-feminist analysis, to show that challenging homophobia can broaden and strengthen the movement for socialism. It was to be a "tool for action".[30] But this did not last.

By 1981 most of the men in the party had all but abandoned this approach and had moved solidly behind the shift to community politics. Some were arguing that "a task for radicals is to make alliances with independent small business as part of our efforts to build an effective and broad gay rights movement."[31] When there was a push to change the date of Mardi Gras to the summer months, lesbians in the party led the opposition, arguing it would depoliticise the event. Johnston and others argued that because Mardi Gras was broader, it had the potential to represent the whole gay community and provide a bigger base to build from.[32]

But this was not the CPA's initial approach to building the movement and building the party. In 1974 Denis Freney described their position. He said it was about organising an activist minority that could bring people in around more left-wing demands and build a stronger, fighting movement. The main job then was to go out and confront those institutions that oppress us, involving mass work such as demonstrations. "We've got to find those demands which are really challenging (not the lowest common denominator)...We've got to start from real, felt oppression and at the same time link it to the real causes."³³

At the height of mobilisations in 1978 the Communist Party activists, instead of trying to push the movement to the left, went with the flow planning festivals instead of riots, building a street party but not the Communist Party.

Peter Murphy strongly protests this interpretation, arguing instead that the CPA was going through its most radical period after 1968, "making a real contribution to progressive social change and linking it to a modern socialist objective". In particular he believes Mardi Gras endures as "a more radical moment" in our society.

More than the future of the struggle for gay rights was at stake for the CPA. Its own future was at risk more generally, its shift within the gay movement was symbolic of the other realignments going on. The party had been shrinking since the end of World War II and in his 1991 autobiography Denis Freney wrote that after a short reprieve in the wake of the sacking of Whitlam, by 1977 the CPA was losing members again. "We had sought to get rid of the dross of the party's Stalinist past", he said, "and to adapt our ideas to feminism and other new movements, but to no avail."

Phil Carswell was more positive about the future. Rather than focus on Russia and the Eastern bloc countries which were "not true socialism", and to the sort of change which would take "further agitation, further social movements", Phil preferred to ask what is the social model we really want? Eurocommunism seemed to beckon. He and others looked to the Italian Communist Party, which had recently increased its parliamentary vote to 30 percent.

But Freney had correctly read the writing on the wall. The CPA survived informally within the short-lived New Left Party. It formally ceased to exist as the CPA in 1991.³⁴

However as far as the gay movement was concerned, for the Communist Party 1980 appeared at first to be the continuation of the 1978-79 upsurge. Analysis of the coverage in *Tribune* showed the years 1978 to 1980 had more articles about gay struggles, book and film reviews than the paper had ever carried. Internally the party was developing its gay policies and held a conference of its own gay members.

They'd seemingly made a breakthrough on the Mardi Gras and looked set to continue to be a strong force within the movement. And yet by 1982 *Tribune* coverage of Gay Liberation had plummeted to two articles for the entire year and, except for the later HIV-AIDS coverage, was to stay that way for much of the decade. Feminism had taken its toll on Gay Liberation, with a majority of women involved in lesbian-only activist groups or in welfare-oriented activities such as Rape Crisis Centres and Halfway Houses. Then came AIDS, which laid waste to a generation of gay men. The HIV-AIDS crisis, however, generated a whole new layer of activists, in groups such as ACT-UP. At one of the first Melbourne meetings, young activist Alison Thorne roused the shocked and despairing attendees with her call to action. She asked the simple question, well what are we going to do? And then began to outline how a campaign would need a publicity group, a health liaison group and so on. Seasoned gay liberationists such as Phil Carswell who gave a lead for much of the response to HIV-AIDS in the coming years, attest that it was her call that started the campaign. In Sydney the CPA played an important role in kickstarting and maintaining the campaign.

THE BATTLE OF IDEAS

Our story of Gay Liberation is set in days of hope. Gay Liberationists, along with their comrades in other spheres, were fighting to make a new revolution. Accordingly they were drawn to the revolutionary social theory: Marxism. "They were heady days," said one. "The pain of self-hate cracked into a thousand pieces. For the first time many of us saw the chance of a new way of living and being."[1] They were times of mass strikes and radicalisation. They were days when revolution was "in the air" and Marxism set the tone among the militant political activists.

As an article in William and John, an early gay magazine, wrote: "True gay liberation cannot be achieved in a capitalist society...Gay people cannot fight alone against capitalism, let alone lead...[they] must fight alongside other radical groups. And that means recognising that the largest constituent group in a fight against capitalism is likely to be the working class."[2]

But other theories soon challenged Marxist ideas. Leading activist Liz Jacka could say that: "The minute you situate women in society as a whole, you realise that the only theory available for understanding society as a whole is Marxism. There just isn't any rival theory."[3] Yet she could quickly add that Marxism was incomplete, that feminism articulated "a rebellion and a whole area of life that's been ignored", namely the personal, whereas she saw Marxism as concentrating on the public sphere.[4] Theories of "autonomy", "identity" and "patriarchy" claimed to fill a gap in Marxism; and increasingly they claimed to be superior to Marxism. As Sandra Bloodworth points out, these ideas become more influential when there are lulls in workers' struggles. Groups who have looked to the working class for support see its strength wane and start to feel more isolated.[5] Such ideas then opened the way for dubious alliances; for example some in the Communist Party began arguing radicals should "make alliances with independent small business as part of our efforts to build an effective and broad gay rights movement."[6]

As well for more and more activists the enemy was no longer capitalism but "patriarchy", or in the unvarnished version, the enemy was men. Similarly, those who argued that all straights oppress all gays, or the lesbian separatists who saw all men and in some cases, heterosexual women also as the enemy, had no way of changing the situation (except through some biological solution) and in the extreme argued for societies without men (even without heterosexual women). As a leading light in the move to Radical lesbianism commented, "As a woman I will never be free, will never divest myself of my oppressive sexist conditioning. Neither can any man divest himself of his oppressive status." An abyss indeed.[7]

Within Gay Liberation, not only were the ideas of autonomy gaining currency, but notions of a gay community began to surface. Initially the left could see the problems with such an approach. Craig Johnston pointed to the way descriptions of community had been used to water down ideas of class difference, that "what we have in common, our sexuality, is supposed to take priority".[8] Di Otto explained the prob-lem with this sort of identity politics. She wrote "We make the mistake of assuming that lesbianism, in itself, is a radical position." That led to supporting a range of events or perspectives just because it was lesbians involved. For Otto, this was "as ludicrous as believing that every working-class person is a communist...it is conservative to ignore the differences such as class and political perspective."[9]

Patriarchy theory and autonomy, however, did gain traction across the left, leading to many debates about combining Marxist and feminist analyses; what became known as "the unhappy marriage of Marxism and feminism".[10] The necessity of permanent autonomous organisation of oppressed groups, rather than seeing independent organising as a tactical question, became the accepted position. The CPA and SWP agreed. The IS argued for the tactical approach from the mid-1970s.[11]

While accepting patriarchy and identity theories don't provide a barrier to activism for reforms of the system, they fall short when it comes to answering the question of how to get rid of oppression. Marxism and class politics offer the strategic insights that we need.

The Socialist Workers Party [35]

The revolutionary upsurge of the late 1960s saw challenges to the political dominance of the Communist Party from newly emerging Trotskyist groups. The CPA was often the first to have raised the political issues, the first to have contact with the activists, but sometimes slow to consolidate. This left space for the development of new political groups such as the SWP. Founding member, John Percy wrote that throughout the second half of the 1960s and the early '70s, the Vietnam War was the key question and our movement had its origins in the campaign against it.[36] "There was a real flowering of protest and rebellion, a new feeling that 'We can change the world'."[37]

Percy wrote of the group's politics. "Our roots were the IWW, the CPA and the early Trotskyist group [the Australian group headed by Nick Origlass], but the direct links were tenuous, so the lessons and experiences of overseas revolutionaries, the Fourth International and especially the US Socialist Workers Party, [both Trotskyist] became more important for us." The Australian group adopted the politics of the Trotskyist groups and refuted the Stalinism of the CPA. They argued that Russia, the Eastern Bloc and China had been arrested in their journey to socialism and were either degenerated or bureaucratically deformed workers' states. The SWP saw countries such as Cuba in a favourable light, though it was very critical of that country's early homophobic practices.[38] The Cuban Revolution of 1959 was an inspirational event for young students like Percy and fed into their support for the Vietnamese struggle against Western imperialist intervention. An audience of 400 at a meeting on Cuba at Sydney University illustrated the Third World radicalism of the time.[39]

The campuses provided the emerging group with most of its new members, while it also attracted some high school students. Ken Davis remembers an SYA-planned national school strike in 1972, where 800-1000 students protested at Sydney Town Hall for political rights and against discrimination. At least four gay groups were set up in high schools, including one at Davis's school where there were also prominent gays on the school staff. The groups joined protests but also invited speakers and on one occasion Davis's school group invited the SYA's Nita Keig to speak on women's liberation and Dennis Altman on Gay Lib. The school did not allow Altman to speak

Resistance was the first of the SWP-related organisations to be established, in 1967, though its founding conference was not until 1970 when 45 members attended. 1972 saw the formation of the Socialist Workers League, as the SWP was then called. So during the beginnings and rise of the Gay Liberation movement, the SWP itself was forming and consolidating.

From the beginning the party supported Women's and Gay Liberation and its members were heavily involved in student politics. For its theory the group drew on the American SWP and promoted its publications. Both groups' theoretical contributions developed the analysis that capitalism was the fundamental cause of gay oppression and that it would take socialism to bring liberation. The gains for gay and women's rights from the Russian Revolution, before Stalin's clampdown, were a key reference point for SWP members.[40] One of their position papers, *The socialist attitude to the homosexual struggle*, argued: "While we can win many important reforms and make significant gains at present, it is only after putting an end to the society which is responsible for perpetuating our oppression through its institutions and its ideology, that we can really conceive of totally eliminating it."[41]

The group's newspaper *Direct Action* appeared in September 1970, the year CAMP was formed. The first article about homosexuality, in July 1971 was an attack on a homophobic, anti-Trotskyist piece in the Maoist paper *Vanguard*. The first comprehensive analysis of Gay Liberation appeared in *Direct Action* in September 1971 and included references to the Russian Revolution, declaring that for the Bolsheviks, "it was quite simply the responsibility of the revolution to eliminate all forms of oppression and discrimination".[42] As *Direct Action* (and much later *Green Left Weekly*) the paper reported and analysed the movement's activities and history, with the number of articles providing a rough barometer of Gay Liberation's fortunes. The SWP often fielded candidates in federal and state elections and party policy on homosexuals was reprinted in the paper as part of the general election platform.[43]

The SWP undertook assessments of its role within GLM. The National Committee's 1973 *Memorandum on the Gay Liberation Movement*, emphasised the importance of linking the gay struggle with that of the working class. Though, as Ken Davis points out, initially it was only seen as a "democratic rights issue". While Gay Liberation was not a key national sphere of work at that time for the group, it had involved a number of members and Gay Pride Week activities had "demonstrated the ability of the movement to mobilise significant numbers in action". It had given the SWP an opportunity to engage with lesbians and gay men and win new people to the group and its socialist analysis. The National Committee proposed that branches be prepared to intervene in future activities.[44] Their analysis at this time proved over-optimistic, as Gay Liberation slumped by the end of 1973.

After some time in the doldrums, the movement started to revive in 1975. SWP student members were part of the gay "push" in the AUS that year, including backing the AUS campus motions and later the organising of and delivering papers at the First National Homosexual Conference. Their involvement continued over the intervening years, and they were well-placed to play an important role when the movement reached a second peak in 1978. SWP members were crucial in establishing the Sydney Gay Solidarity Group to organise the International Day of Solidarity on June 24, which ended with the Mardi Gras. Party activists also played a major role in the anti-Mary Whitehouse (anti-Festival of Light) national campaign that same year.[45]

The SWP took 1978 very seriously indeed; its lesbian and gay membership had grown from around 14 activists in 1975 to the high forties in 1978.[46] The upsurge of 1978 saw the SWP buoyant, predicting a vibrant movement poised for victories. Allen Myers, one of the party's leaders, wrote that they wanted the SWP to be an integral part of the movement, with a more organised party intervention, providing political leadership. "As a minimum target, every branch should be working towards the establishment of a functioning gay fraction."[47] The SWP leadership argued that the GLM was moving left, organising to build mass actions rather than relying on parliamentarians, seeking allies in the organised working class and overall adopting a militant program. The Party expected sharpening class conflict under the Fraser government to bring a test of strength between workers and the ruling class. Every victory by the bosses, whether it was against gays or any other oppressed group, Myers argued, would be a defeat for the working class just as much as a wage cut or a rise in unemployment. The struggle for homosexual liberation was part of the workers' struggle.

1979 saw a significant redirection of the SWP's activity, heavily influenced by the American group. The party wanted members to be a key force in the unions in the face of the projected increase in industrial action, so the leadership argued it was time for the SWP to "turn to industry". Adopted by some groups on the left in a mistakenly optimistic analysis of the times, the policy saw placing most party members in blue-collar jobs as a way to build the party and build the class struggle. Lesbian and gay members would be meeting some of the hundreds of thousands of working class homosexuals who could be won to the fight for union anti-discrimination policies and the more general struggle for liberation. The party argued that this was "a necessary part of the Trotskyist understanding of the need to turn the trade unions into fighting instruments of the oppressed." It was a turn to the union rank and file through militant mass action, not doing deals or compromising with the union leadership.

Nonetheless, during 1979 the SWP had a full calendar of campaigns and protests around gay issues. These included NSW pickets demanding the government deliver on law reform; a Drop the Charges campaign arising from the 1978 protests; and a demonstration against Newcastle's Star Hotel's refusal to serve gay clients.[48] There were events in other states and lesbian custody rights became an issue. Optimistic references to the planned 1980 Summer Offensive campaign and adoption of the SWP's *Strategy for homosexual liberation* policy rounded out the year.[49]

Reflecting a long-running debate between the more conservative and more radical wings of the movement, the *Strategy* argued that if gay rights activists were to bring about substantial changes, "playing things quietly and confining the movement to lobbying respectable politicians", was not the way forward. It was a strategy for defeat. Instead lesbians and gays needed "a fighting program" to defend their rights, especially in the face of any prospective right-wing offensive.[50]

The SWP saw itself as politically positioned between the left reformism of the CPA and the alleged ultra-left tactics of groups such as the International Socialists. The *Strategy* argued the tactics of both reformism and ultra-leftism could only end in defeat. Instead, the SWP posed what it said was "a quite different way forward, a strategy of mass action, of mobilising as many people as possible in demonstrations focussed on specific and uncompromising demands." This would be the way to take lesbian and gay demands into the working class. It was only Marxists (the SWP here claiming the mantle solely for itself) who understood that the struggles against oppression were an inseparable part of the class struggle.[51]

The SWP was confident it could reach out to new social layers and draw them into action and draw them into its project of building for a revolutionary party. During the course of such struggles the group believed that masses of gays would accept the party's explanations of the "profound stake which homosexuals have in the socialist revolution". However a combination of the SWP's sharp turn to industry, its rapid reallocation of many members to work in the growing anti-uranium movement, and a significant drop in gay activism put paid to such optimistic predictions. There was an exodus of gay members and the Party's work around lesbian and gay issues fell dramatically. Again, as with the CPA, the AIDS crisis took its toll of members, but it did propel others into action later in the 1980s and new gay members were won to the SWP.

The International Socialists[52]

The smallest of the three significant groups and the latest onto the political scene was the International Socialists (IS). Forming as a small discussion group at the end of 1971, during 1972 its membership stayed at around 20-30. While there was quick turnover, the group had started to clarify its political stance. By November 1975 membership was still low (~20), but in the wake of the November 11 constitutional crisis, the numbers went up fairly rapidly to around 70. The group was still thinly spread across south eastern Australia, but it felt politically confident enough to establish itself as a national organisation with agreed upon politics.[53]

Most important initially for the group was the small, but politically coherent, student club at Monash University, the Revolutionary Communists or RevComs (1972). Although not formally part of the IS at the beginning, they shared opposition to Australian nationalism and support for workers' struggles. Their anti-nationalist stance, as well as their support for Women's and Gay Liberation brought them into conflict with the more prominent Maoist students. However as Tess Lee Ack recalls, "There was only ever a handful of RevComs, but we had quite a lot of influence among left-wing students and by 1974 were pretty much the leading group on the campus left." Tess herself was elected to the Monash Association of Students' political wing, the Public Affairs Committee and was active in the Women's and Gay Liberation clubs. She helped write and put out the Rev-Coms newsletter *Hard Lines* and gained a reputation as a leading student activist.[54]

Hard Lines supported Gay Liberation, with the RevComs standing on joint election tickets alongside Gay and Women's Liberation candidates. The newsletter advertised Sexuality Week events, sexual liberation forum and promoted 1973 Gay

Pride week. More generally the club campaigned against the homophobia and sexism of the administration and right-wing students. Promoting Gay Pride, *Hard Lines* talked of the nationwide events which would involve "more homosexuals in Australia than any other organised activity". The week would involve those heterosexuals "who identify with the gay movement against the oppression of homosexuals – that's important as it is too easy to view all heterosexuals as our oppressors when these are people who are questioning and changing their attitudes towards us." *Hard Lines* also campaigned for the AUS pro-gay motions in 1975.

The RevComs were involved in initiating the country's first "Homosexuals and Society" course. It included talks about homosexual liberation, socialism and women's liberation. The course itself, even though it was non-accredited, drew the ire of Vice Chancellor Matheson outraged that students would organise such a course on campus. It was a threat, he claimed, to the very core of "university values". The series went ahead.[55]

One of the founding members of the IS, Janey Stone, had been involved in Women's Liberation in the USA, at Berkeley, as well as being briefly in Paris during some of the 1968 upheavals. This "American connection" partly explains the readiness with which the IS took up the gay cause. On her return to Australia, she initiated Women's Liberation at Melbourne University alongside several lesbians, including Sue Jackson and future AUS Women's Officer Laurie Bebbington. The first Sexuality Week on campus featured a dinner which Stone chaired. She believes it may have been the first time openly lesbian or gay speakers had appeared at Melbourne University. "We felt like we were breaking new ground." Amongst some of the liberal-minded magazines was *Dissent*, where Stone's article "The Biology of Sex and Sexuality" was published. Both Lee Ack and Stone were at Melbourne's first gay demo on Swanston Street in December 1972. It was a politically charged time, with the prospect of a Labor government coming to power after 23 years of conservative rule. Off-campus, the IS was slowly building a base.

Initially it had a strong trade union and workplace focus. However in the first issue of its paper *The Battler* in November 1972, there was a full page article, "What is The Party Line on Love?" In it Janey Stone wrote of the rich humanitarian tradition of revolutionaries such as Alexandra Kollontai and the lessons of the Russian Revolution, as well as welcoming the contributions of Women's and Gay Liberation. She added, "We believe that revolutionaries should be *sex-affirming*."[56]

The next issue of the paper wasn't until October 1974, coinciding with a period of downturn in the gay movement. However members of the IS were active in their unions. Tess Lee Ack and Tom O'Lincoln were in the rank and file group, Teacher Action. This group successfully argued for the Victorian Secondary Teachers Association to establish women's and later, homosexual subcommittees. These subcommittees were tasked to come up with anti-discrimination policies and practices and were open to rank and file members.[57]

In 1977 the paper began to include articles about gay liberation, starting with reports on the Greg Weir campaign. When the movement hit its peak in 1978, *The Battler* ran articles on Mardi Gras, the "Gays at Work" national homosexual conference and the protests against Mary Whitehouse.

1978 was also the first year the group had a number of lesbian and gay members who could attend many of the gay-only groups. With the increase in membership, the IS could stage a serious intervention into the 1978 protests and Homosexuals at Work conference as well as the 1981 Socialism and Homosexuality forum. In Melbourne as part of the campaign against Mary Whitehouse, Janey Stone chaired the public meeting and IS members were part of the demonstrations around the country. At the Melbourne anti-Festival of Light campaign forum, Tom O'Lincoln challenged the ALP speaker Gareth Evans to come to the rally. Evans said unfortunately he couldn't, he'd be addressing a meeting in Ballarat on "the future of socialism"! The group held public branch meetings on Gay Liberation and at one time ran a debate, *Which way forward for the Australian gay movement*, in its theoretical journal. Contributions came from independent activist Michael Hurley, Phil Carswell from the CPA and Graham Willett, then an IS member.[58] Coverage of lesbian and gay issues continued in the paper until 1985. After a break of three years when the paper became a more theoretical publication, there was greater coverage in *The Socialist* of HIV-AIDS and ACT-UP protests, many involving IS activists.

What was significant about the IS, as compared to the CPA and the SWP was its more critical view of autonomous organising.[59] In a paper to the Socialism and Homosexuality Conference, then-member Alison Thorne put the IS position: "In the early 1970s the autonomous gay movement played a vital role in advancing the struggle for gay liberation. It contributed to the growth of gay pride...it explored and advanced the understanding of sexual politics, especially of the relationship between gay liberation and socialism." As the movement declined, however, it had became more inward looking and lost direction. Clinging to autonomous organising "always and everywhere", the IS argued, closed off possibilities for the movement to grow.[60]

The group favoured more united front work in the vein of the anti-Festival of Light campaign, including opposing the later de-politicisation of Mardi Gras. The IS pointed to the missed opportunity arising out of the "Drop the Charges" campaign against the police attacks at Mardi Gras. The July demonstration in Sydney immediately after Mardi Gras was the biggest protest for gay rights that the country had seen and it was joined by trade unionists, straights (heterosexuals), political groups and other campaign groups. The arrests of gays were seen as an attack on everyone's rights. Then-International Socialist member Di Minnis explained that in building for the demonstration, activists (gay and straight) were able to win over fellow workers to the need to fight for gay rights.[61]

The IS, like the other left groups, argued for building support within the unions through gay caucuses, rank and file groups and solidarity work with other struggles. The necessity of building a revolutionary party out of the struggles of the day, was pushed for by the group. Coalitions, united fronts and links between workers and oppressed groups, IS members argued at the Socialism and Homosexuality conference, important as they are, could not in themselves give the necessary coordination and leadership required to overthrow capitalism. The state of the movement, the group said, only served to underline the need to build a party which could unite the isolated areas of struggles.[62]

As the movement crumbled, the class struggle declined and HIV-AIDS took its toll, the International Socialists, like the rest of the Left, proved too weak to hold most of their lesbian and gay members against the rightward pull. As the left struggled to adjust, the casualties were high. Lesbians and gays, many of whom had ended up in demanding welfare and policy jobs, joined the general drift away from revolutionary politics and left the groups they'd so enthusiastically joined in the 1970s. The IS was also caught up in two major splits. Socialist Alternative, a successor to the IS has since become the biggest group on the left and a key organisation in the Equal Love campaign. It took consistent theorising around the questions of gay liberation, autonomy and identity politics, as well as significant involvement on the campuses, for Socialist Alternative to rebuild a layer of committed left-wing gay activists, people committed to building both the campaigns and a group of revolutionary socialists, throughout the 1990s and 2000s.

CHAPTER 7

REVOLUTION IS FOR US![1]

The history of the struggle for gay liberation is inspiring. It had a transformational impact on millions of lesbians and gay men around the world. As well, like the Women's Liberation and Black rights movements of the day, it changed the lives of others.

We didn't first take to the streets in 1969 at Stonewall – or at the Mardi Gras in 1978 in Australia. There is a rich history, stretching back to the late 1800s, early 1900s in Germany, shortly after the word "homosexual" was coined. For much of this time the organised left has rallied to support lesbians and gays in their campaigns for equal rights – and liberation.

The first politician anywhere in the world to speak in parliament for the rights of gays was August Bebel, leader of the German Social Democrats, who addressed the German Reichstag on January 13, 1898. In defending Oscar Wilde in the SPD's paper, Bebel also argued against the notion of 'natural' and 'unnatural' sexuality. Examining attitudes to homosexual behaviour in those earlier societies, as well as those of his day, he concluded that "moral attitudes are historical phenomena". That is they changed as societies changed, something which was decided by people and their society, not some eternal position.[1]

The left brought analysis, organisation and a focus on what united us in our fight against the common enemy, capitalism. It argued the case for total social change – for revolution, not just reforms. It has had a political influence far beyond its actual numbers, initiating some of the major actions and left activists were founding members of many of the organisations, movements and campaigns.

Understanding why capitalist society has oppressed and repressed homosexuality was – and is still today – one of the left's most important contributions to the struggle for gay liberation. Understanding where oppression comes from, what are the forces we have to fight determine what sorts of movements we build, what allies we seek and ultimately how we can fundamentally change the world we live in.

Left groups argued that "Gay oppression is an adjunct of women's oppression and women's oppression springs from the demands of class society. Without the abolition of class there can be no liberation for women or gays."[2] Abolishing class society, the left said, could only come from winning a revolution of the kind that happened in Russia in 1917. And the force that could achieve such a revolution, the Socialist Homosexuals explained in their manifesto, was the working class, "the only class with the potential to lead a revolution because of its size, organisation and base at the point of production". Young workers and activists of the 60s drew on this tradition as they challenged the system. And it is this – Marxist – tradition, that enabled the newly emerging gay liberationists to explain homosexual oppression, to organise against it and fight for liberation.

Co-founder of Gay Liberation, Jim Fourratt rightly captured the spirit of the age when he proclaimed, "There was going to be a revolution, and we were going to be a part of it."[3]

ENDNOTES

Introduction
1 Sydney Gay Liberation leaflet March 1972 *We are your worst fears...your best fantasies*. Handed out at IWD
2 Walter, 1980, p.17
3 Marilyn Lake as quoted in John Murphy, 2000 p.3

Chapter 1
1 A longer version of this chapter was published under the same title in the State Library of Victoria's journal *The La Trobe Journal*, no.83, May 2011 pp.107-115. I have made significant alterations to the original.
2 Vigilant "Loves Coming of Age", *The Westralian* 2 March 1917 p.2. The following quotes about Carpenter's book are from this review.
3 The quote is from Engels *Origin of the Family* where he discusses what relations between people will be like under a future socialist society. Other quotes from Vigilant about Oscar Wilde *Westralian Worker* August 1917 http://john.curtin.edu.au/fitzgerald/collection/pen4.html (accessed 15 August 2010).
4 *Ross's Monthly*, Vol 2, no. 21 (August 1917), p.15. The monthly publication had close relations with the Victorian Socialist Party and often ran articles by its members, while the VSP's *The Socialist* regularly advertised *Ross's* magazine and its articles.
5 Carleton, 2005, p.2
6 Lambrick wrote a two-part article on the times; the quote is from 24 January. *The Socialist* 17 January 1919, p. 3 and 24 January 1919, p.2.
7 Initially the Australian Communist Party – ACP, I have used the more familiar Communist Party of Australia – CPA – throughout. The CPA dissolved itself in 1991, but two parties – the Communist Party (previously the SPA) and the Communist Party of Australia (Marxist-Leninist) – currently claim descendancy from the original CPA. See O'Lincoln 2009 and Macintyre, 1995.
8 Macintyre, 1995 p.104.
9 The Sydney-based Australian Socialist Party (ASP) played a bigger role in forming the CPA, but it had earlier dissolved itself into the CPA.

10   This is a controversial position on Russia which this chapter cannot address. I refer readers to Tony Cliff *State Capitalism in Russia*. London Pluto 1974. Writings on this are available at the Marxist Internet Archive www.marxists.org , www.swp.org.uk, www.socialistworker.org or www.sa.org.au .

11   As quoted in German, 2007, p.180

12   Burgmann 1985, p.135 "Early in 1905, Tom Mann, who had long been despairing of the Labor Party, resigned his position as organiser and resolved on promoting even more determined socialist organisation in Victoria. In March 1905 he formed a Social Questions Committee, which launched the Victorian Socialist Party (VSP) in September 1905, a spectacularly successful organisation that could boast, within a couple of years, a membership of 200 in Melbourne alone."

13   *Adelaide Advertiser* 5.9.1908, p.5. Initially it was thought that homosexuality was rarely covered by the mainstream press, but more recent research continues to discover a richer history. I am indebted to Robert French's initial listing of newspaper references, "Between the Broadsheets" and the later research by Gary Jaynes at ALGA.

14   *The Socialist* 15 December 1906, p. 3, 22 December 1906, p.5; Several verses of Oscar Wilde's The Ballad of Reading Gaol are reprinted in *The Socialist* 2 February 1907, p.4.

15   *The Socialist* 20 October 1906, p.4. Edwards was, in fact, Australian born and had dressed as a man so successfully that she married several times. See Chesser, 2008.

16   Hobsbawm, 1982 pp.216-9

17   Pankhurst *The Communist* 24 December 1920, p.1

18   Macintyre, 1995 p.26-7

19   Pankhurst, 1920; Morgan *The Communist* 5 August 1921, p. 6

20   Phil Griffiths Women and the CPA: 1920-1945. 1998 http://www.philgriffiths.id.au/writings/Aust_hist_old.html

21   Macintyre, 1995, p.264

22   Damousi, 1994 p.135

23   O'Lincoln, 2009, p.53; Mcintyre, 1995, pp.110-111

24   Willett, 2008; 2009. Collinson went to the UK in 1964 and never returned to live in Australia.

25   Nicole Moore, 2012 ; *Banned books in Australia. A comprehensive survey of book censorship in Australia from settlement to the twenty-first century*. Exhibition, conference and book. Melbourne University Press. 2010.

26   The ban was more of a blow than it may seem at first as many Australian books were actually published in the UK.

27   http://www.austlit.edu.au/specialistDatasets/Banned/ ;. http://www.naa.gov.au/about-us/research-grants/margaret-george-award/former/moore-paper-2004-old.aspx (accessed 15 August 2010); Nicole Moore, 2012

28   Damousi, 1994, p.72

Endnotes

29 Willett et al, 2012; Clarsen, 2008, pp.104-119
30 Monte, quoted in Ford, 1996, p.115; Monte was famous because she was 102 when she publicly 'came out'. Willett et al, 2012
31 *Tribune* 25.10.1932
32 Ferrier, 1999 pp.44-45
33 Wotherspoon, 2009 p.44. Wotherspoon also notes Kylie Tennant's 1957 novel *Tell Morning This*, where the Archibald Fountain in Kings Cross is 'outed' as a homosexual 'cruising' site.
34 The great contribution by CPA writers, especially the women, to literature and theatre and the breaking with the restrictive stereotypes in the period from 1930s through to the 1960s is covered particularly by Carole Ferrier and Michelle Arrow (see Bibliography). Another study of Devanny's work also cites her novel *Riven*, with an "ambiguous" heroine, Lillith. Paxton, 2008
35 It was Friedrich Wolf, a German Communist playwright, who, in 1928, first proclaimed: *Kunst ist Waffe!* (art is a weapon).
36 Macintyre, 1995 p.319-320
37 Rex Chiplin was especially outraged by these imports. Headlining his article in November 1953, "I spent a week in a literary sewer", he wrote, "I've been wading through the pornography, sex, sadism, brutality and illiteracy sold each week on Australian newsstands under the guise of 'books' and 'comics'..." *Tribune* 11.11.1953. Queensland TLC campaign *Tribune* 20.8.1952; 27.8.1952
38 Ferres, 1994. Devanny had spoken publicly on the subject of literature and censorship in her 1935 Presidential address to the Writers' League, at various meetings and in a radio broadcast, "The Censorship of Books." In the drafts of Devanny's speech, references to the suppression of Radclyffe Hall's *The Well of Loneliness* are struck out, though the comments remain as general observations. The Well "expos[es] the injustices of our benighted civilisation, aiming to provide a better understanding of certain forces inherent in mankind or womankind."
39 It is possible that this refers to a New York court order against all of Wilhelm Reich's personal collection of books. Long time sexual reform activist in Germany, Reich escaped Germany to the US where he maintained his activism there. Reich was jailed in the US in 1957 for his activities around sexual reform and died a year later while still in jail.

In another 1953 article detailing the feared anti-Communist, homophobe, Senator Joseph McCarthy's criminal activities, it was noted that he lived with his administrative assistant, Ray Kiermas. But there is no suggestion in the article that McCarthy was gay and it is possible Kiermas just lived in the same apartment block as McCarthy – an apartment block the Senator owned. There have been other suggestions that McCarthy was gay. *Tribune* 31 March 1953, p. 9; Mazzell – *Tribune* 5.8.1953

40 Wotherspoon, 1991 p.81

41 O'Lincoln, 2011 p.132
42 Wotherspoon, 1991, p.81
43 "Given a lead, bodgies won't be conscripts". *Tribune*, 22 February 1951, p. 6; "Why the attacks on bodgies and widgies?" *Tribune* 9.12.1951, p.8
44 Wotherspoon, 1991, p.103 – *Adelaide Truth* 31.1.1948, also in Sydney and Melbourne editions of the paper. The Kinsey book on women's sexuality was described by *Melbourne Truth* as "Kinsey Book. Muckraking libel on sex" *Melbourne Truth* 29.8.1953 p.1,4
45 Willett, 2004, p.23. It was also reported in *The Australian*.
46 Gowland Interview
47 Ciszek, 2006, p..28
48 Carswell. Interview
49 Denis Freney "Gay Liberation" *Tribune* 26 May 1971, p. 6.

Chapter 2

1 *Melbourne Community Voice* 2.7.2009 p.3
2 "Despite Governor Phillip's enthusiasm, however, it was four decades before anti-sodomy laws were systematically implemented in the new colonies. Only in 1828 did the first hangings for sodomy take place in NSW and Van Dieman's Land. The majority of sodomy trials in NSW before the middle of the nineteenth century happened in just one decade, the 1830s, and the last execution occurred the year before transportation ceased in 1839. In Van Dieman's Land, the penal colony for recalcitrant prisoners from other Australian colonies, where transportation continued longer, the incidence of execution was higher than in NSW and lasted into the 1860s. During the 1840s, official reports started moralising about lesbian activity among convict women and there were cases of women being punished for such behaviour in the female prisons." (Morgain)
3 In 1904 Anna Ruhling addressed a women's movement meeting "What interest does the women's movement have in the homosexual question". In Blasius and Phelan, 1997, pp. 143-150
4 Chudacoff, 1999, p.114. In 1895 a group of gay men with around 100 members formed the Cercle Hermaphroditus, in New York. It appears to have been largely social, though other sources suggest that its aim was "to unite for defense against the world's bitter persecution". Earl Lind, who described himself as an hermaphrodite, founded the group; later he wrote about his life in what may be the first autobiography of an hermaphrodite. http://lgbts.yale.edu/history-lgbts-yale
5 Willett,2009, p.115
6 Marilyn Lake as quoted in John Murphy, 2000 p.3
7 ibid

Endnotes

8 Murphy, 2000 p.28
9 Ibid p.29
10 ibid p.5-6
11 Ferrier, 1999 p.6
12 ibid
13 As reported by *Nation* 21.5.60, after the event. In Gerster & Jan Bassett 1991, p.40
14 Moore, Clive 2000, pp.85-6
15 Timmons, 1990, p.143 As Hay became more involved in his Mattachine work, he became more concerned that his homosexuality would negatively affect the Communist Party. Hay recommended his own expulsion as a homosexual which was refused by the Party, but both agreed to expulsion as a 'security risk', while he was announced with some fanfare as a "Lifelong Friend of the People".
It was author Donald Webster Cory (the pseudonym of Edward Sagarin) who first described homosexuals as a class in his 1951 book *The Homosexual in America: a subjective approach*.
16 D'Emilio, 1983 p.67
17 Mattachine was more closed than later groups, initially operating within a "cell" structure like that of Communist Party, until the change in leadership. Within a few years its structure and principles were watered down when an anti-Communist grouping of members took over the organisation. This led to a dramatic fall in membership from around 2000 to the tens, scattered around the country. See D'Emilio, 1983 pp.57-91
18 Belinda Baldwin, nd, "1/1/67:The Black Cat Riots", http://www.glreview.com/article.php?articleid=1010
19 Johnson, 2004; Hay ,1996; Timmons, 1990; Baldwin op cit
20 Lesbian Manifesto – reprinted in *Lesbian Voices* Vol IV no.2. p.2 1981. Originally published in *The Ladder*, the DOB's monthly publication. Gallo, 2006.
21 Liz Highleyman, nd "It didn't start with Stonewall" http://bayoccupride.com/it-didnt-start-with-stonewall/
22 Wotherspoon, 1991, pp.18-19
23 When the ALP was in power in the late 40s, then Immigration Minister Arthur Calwell issued a pamphlet called *Danger to Australia*, part of the orchestrated anxiety of the Cold War. Alomes et al, 1984, p.9
24 Davison, 2010 p.19, Delaney's "homosexuality as the greatest menace" was reported in the *SMH* 28.6.1958
25 Not that he had anything to fear on this score. As *Tribune* reported, the state Premier was quick to scotch any proposals for a Royal Commission into the force and earned the praise of Delaney. "We wonder why?" *Tribune* 29.4.53
26 *Sydney Daily Telegraph* 6.12.53

27 Cranenburgh, 2010 p.37
28 ibid p.65
29 *Canberra Times* 25.8.52; Church sex report *Sydney Mirror (SDM)* 25.5.1956; Church recommends reform *People* 11.7.1956.
30 Weeks, 1977, pp.176-8. However Weeks quotes author Michael Schofield (aka Gordon Westwood) as commenting that while the law had changed things "only a little", but "I think it was vital and it opens the door to serious change in the future." (p.178)
31 *People* 16.10.1957. *People* became more a more racy publication later on.
32 "Soviet acted on their Kinsey Report" *Tribune* 2.9.1953, p.6. In 1959 there was a long article condemning religious crusader Billy Graham who had visited Australia several times for his puritanical and bourgeois views on the family and the home. Author (Reverend Victor James!) still upholds the importance of the family, but portrays the working class family attacked by capitalism. *Tribune* 12.2.1959
33 Half-Humanity column by Freda Brown *Tribune* 2.1.1952 p.7
34 *Tribune* 14.5.1958; See also Blears, 2002. The Eureka Youth League promoted healthy, exercise-filled lifestyles.
35 Stone and Stone, 1945 p.237
36 Davison, 2005 pp.58-61
37 ibid; Rod Anderson interview
38 Ferrier, 1999, p.105
39 Anderson, 2006 p.56, 59
40 Damousi, 1994, p.135
41 Davison, 2005 pp.52, 58-59.
42 Bill Leslie interview
43 Willett, 2011
44 Anderson returned to Australia in 1978 and still considers himself a socialist though he never rejoined.
45 Weeks, 1977, p.190

Chapter 3
1 www.marxists.org/history/etol/writers/birchall/1983/01/gorz.htm
2 Gerster and Bassett, 1991 p.41
3 O'Lincoln, 2009.
4 In October 1979 the Victorian Gay Trade Unionist Group sent a letter to the SPA requesting information on party's attitude to homosexuality. Their reply

was: "So far the Socialist Party has not determined a policy on this question, nor have we published any articles in *The Socialist* or elsewhere relating to it..."

5   At the time the SWP was called Resistance, then SWL. Resistance remained the youth group. The IS was known as Socialist Workers Action Group or SWAG.from 1973 to 1975

6   O'Lincoln, 2009 p.142-3

7   Denis Freney, 1991, p.261, Denis had spent time overseas, belonging to the Pabloite tendency of the Trotskyist movement. Led by Michel Pablo, this group had published a pamphlet on women which was circulated by the Sydney Trotskyists in 1966. http://www.marxists.org/archive/pablo/1960/xx/women.htm

8   http://indigenousrights.net.au/section.asp?sID=33

9   See *Tribune* coverage; Wood 2013.

10 Freney was right about the portrayal of nudes in a positive light, but an article critical of double standards in 1964 reprinted two pictures of semi-naked women from the popular press of the day. Denis Freney, 1991 p. 252; Beardsley drawings *Tribune* 10.12.1969 p.2; "It's Mayday, Man!" *Tribune* 30.5.1969, p.1

11 Letter to the Editor. *Tribune* 24.2.65 p.7 *Neue Rheinische Zeitung*: newspaper produced by Marx and Engels in 1848.

12 "Young Oz editors jailed. Obscenity charge; but was it really politics?" *Tribune* 30.9.1964 p.3

13 "'You grubs are here to learn how to kill': a letter from a NS trainee", *Tribune* 21.12.1965 p.9; "Sniggers for Sister George", *Tribune* 3.8.1966 p.6; "'Liar, provocateur' in 'exposure' case: Judge slams policeman's evidence", *Tribune* 17.8.1966 p.11

14 Willett, 2000

15 Gordon Hawkins "Homosexuality. Australia's greatest menace?" *The Bulletin* 8.5.1965 pp.21-2. Re: the judges, see Willett, 2000

16 This fine sentiment didn't stop the *SMH* several years later refusing an ad for CAMP, nor refusing to review Dennis Altman's book. *SMH* 29 July 1967 p.2

17 "The All-Male Ball. And then they started throwing punches!" *Impact* 16.12.1967 p.6. Despite at least 16 fights being broken up, the dinner table overturned, one man described the ball as being "wonderful".

18 All reported in *Lots Wife*

19 Willett, 2002. p.6. The *Australian* reported 293:97, while *Farrago* 281:98

20 *Lots Wife* 7.8.1964. The letters in response, only one of which was anonymous, supported the "Homosexual Villain" and opposed the sentiments of the one person who was against homosexuality. The letters appeared in *Lots Wife* of 17.9.64, 2.10.64 and 21.10.64. To my knowledge no one has claimed to be this anonymous homosexual, nor has their identity been revealed by anyone else.

21 Gerster and Bassett, 1991, pp 55-7 Wendy Bacon faced many charges, almost all of which were dropped. However in one case Bacon who had published a poem called "Cunt is a Christian Word" turned up to court wearing a nun's habit emblazoned with slogans. She got an additional charge of "exhibiting an obscene publication". The UNSW student publication was variously *Tharunka*, *Thorunka* and *Thor*.

22 Information in the following paragraphs comes from: Hall, 1998 pp.186-202

23 Hall comments that it had taken Spry a "very long time" to detect this threat in 1963 given he'd been appointed in 1950.

24 Barbara Farrelly quotes Jan Hillier, one of Melbourne's well-known lesbians, who used to go to El Sombrero. It was "the most wonderful place to go, run by an Italian mamma who did great spaghetti with a crowd composed of "prostitutes, lesbians, drag queens and gangsters". "Lest we forget" *LOTL* July 1998 pp.20-1. Willett, et al 2011 pp 886-88

25 D'Emilio, 1983

26 http://www.bilerico.com/2008/02/the_1965_deweys_lunch_counter_sitins.php ; http://transgriot.blogspot.com.au/2007/10/1965-deweys-lunch-counter-sit-it.html ; See Stein 2000

27 "1/1/67: The Black Cat Riots" Belinda Baldwin, http://www.glreview.com/article.php?articleid=1010 The following paragraphs about the Black Cat riots and the situation in the US are from this article.

28 http://www.generationonfire.com/fouratt.html

29 Teal, 1971 p.19

30 "Gay Revolution Comes Out," *Rat*, August 12-26, 1969, p. 7. There are many histories of Stonewall. See Carter, 2004; Duberman 1994; Teal, 1971

31 Willett, 2011 HLRS

32 Carberry, 2011

33 Burgmann, 1993, p.77; See also Kaplan, 1996

34 Wills, 1981 p.21

35 ibid

36 Burgmann, 1993, p.81

37 Wills, 1981

38 Betty Friedan notoriously labelled lesbians as the "lavender menace" for the women's movement. She was to change her position and publicly welcome lesbians to the movement.

39 Hobart Women's Action Group 1973

40 Ross, 2010. Interviews with Phyllis Papps and Francesca Curtis. The following quotes come from both these sources.

41 ALM leaflet 1970 p.2..

42 *Bulletin* 2.12.1972 p.29

43 Papps interview.

Endnotes

44 *ALM Newsletter* 1972a p.1
45 Ross, 2010; Papps and Curtis interviews.
46 The following draws on Willett 2000, pp.33-52; Ware 2010; *CAMP Ink*; Widdup, 1976; Foss 1973
47 Janet Hawley "Homosexuals form group aimed at ending aura of mystique, secrecy" *The Australian* (Sydney edition only) 10.9.1970, p.3; Janet Hawley "Couples" *The Australian* 19.9.1970 p.14-15
48 Foss, 1973
49 Poll, 1970
50 *Camp Ink* Dec 71/Jan 72 pp 13-17
51 *Bulletin* 10.10.1971 p.32
52 "Sydney Scene" *Camp Ink* Vol 2, no.1 November 1971 p.9

Chapter 4

1 *Sydney Gay Liberation Newsletter* Vol 1 no, 3 September 1972. Comment from a newcomer after a Gay Liberation meeting. Reassured that Gay Lib wouldn't just demonstrate, "instead, the sane, logical point was put forward that it should be something worthwhile to demonstrate about... We live in an age of demonstrations."
2 Altman, 1971 p.11
3 This was handed out as a leaflet in Sydney. Shelley's article, initially published in *Rat*, 24 February 1970, is reprinted in Jay and Young, 1972, pp.31-34.
4 Wolf, 2009 p.126 .
5 Martha Shelley interview, ref. http://www.smith.edu/libraries/libs/ssc/vof/transcripts/Shelley.pdf
   In DOB Shelley took the initiative, speaking to one other DOB member who endorsed it. The local leadership of Mattachine was not in favour of the proposal, but did tell Shelley that she could put it to a meeting of members.
6 http://www.generationonfire.com/fouratt.html
7 Wolf, 2009 p.128
8 Altman, 1971, p.11 Includes the poem "Flaming Faggots" by Ken Pitchford. Poem reprinted
   http://tawkwardturtle.tumblr.com/post/21582219061/flaming-faggots ; Jay & Allen, 1972, p.217
9 One young woman who tried to join ALM was knocked back because she was under 21. So she began handing out her own leaflets on Flinders Street Station. When the push to form GLM groups on campus she was one of the founding members of Melbourne's GLM.
10 Letter from a Campus CAMP member to *Honi Soit* March 1971
11 *On Dit* Vol 39 no.11, 30 June 1971 pp.4-5

12 *Tribune* 26 May 1971 p.6; *Time* magazine did run an article "The Homosexual: Newly visible, newly understood" in October 1969, after Stonewall. While it mentioned Gay Liberation, its main focus was an overview of the situation of homosexuals and the need to become more accepting. Christobel Poll's article in *The Old Mole*, 26 October 1970, while titled Gay Liberation, took a 'homophile' rather than revolutionary approach.

Thompson, 1985, pp. 36-7.Two Gay Liberation Front leaflets entitled 'Gay is Good', Paul Foss and John Lee suggest, were circulating in late 1970 or early 1971. One had a contact name, but no actual group has ever been identified; it is mostly an attack on CAMP. Internal checking of the document, authorised by Bruce Asher, gives an address for GLF as 67 Glebe Point Road. This means it cannot be any earlier than 1972, not 1970 as Foss claims. The other is a reprint of Martha Shelley's iconic "Gay is Good". Shelley's article was also in *Playgue*, a short-lived radical magazine. It is possible Shelley's "Gay is Good" was circulated earlier than 1972 in Australia by Women's Liberation.

13 Bell,1975 p.7. These first Gay Liberationists included Tony Crewes, Dennis Altman (then a lecturer at Sydney University), John Lee, Mim Loftus, Pam Stone/Stein and Meaghan Morris. Others mentioned by Sue Wills included Robert Tucker, John Storey. Dennis gave three talks – one at CAMP, one at Women's Liberation Centre and one at the Third World Bookshop – all in Sydney.

John Lee remembers the first Gay Liberation meetings were about equal women and men. All the quotes from John Lee come from an interview with him by Robert French, 24 February 1991, the recording and transcript held at Pride History, Sydney.

14 *Camp Ink* Vol 1, no. 1, p.2 November 1970
15 Altman, 1979, p.15
16 Perth had Campus CAMP whose leading light was a radical and saw himself more as a Gay Lib activist than holding to CAMP's politics.
17 Gay Lib in Adelaide – inaugural mtg – 23 August 1972 *On Dit* 24.8.1972 p.9
18 *Sydney Gay Liberation Newsletter* Vol.1, no.2. August 1972
19 *Gay Rays* no.1 December 1972.
20 *Gay Rays* no.1 December 1972.
21 "Gay Liberation…Welcomes new members". Sydney c. March 1973
22 Wills, 1994
23 Gay Lib grows angry at ABC *Age* 13.7.1972
24 *Sydney Gay Liberation Newsletter* Vol 1 no.1 July 1972
25 Foss, 1973
26 Gowland, 1973 p.8; Thompson, 1985 p.17
27 "Zapping the psychiatrists." *Tribune* 14-20.8.1973, p.12
28 *Sydney Gay Liberation Newsletter* Vol.1, no.2. August 1972. McConaghy continued to support such treatment of gays throughout his life.

Endnotes

29 *Gay Rays* no.1 December 1972. One can only assume that "homosexual" apples was a reference to the apple in the biblical Garden of Eden, the symbol of temptation. To my knowledge, no explanation from the organisers of the demo has surfaced.

30 ibid

31 It was thanks to the SWP's Direct Action coverage of IWD that this historic moment was recorded. *Direct Action* 16.3.1972, p.16

32 Gowland, 1973 p.8. Mention of Gay Lib at the Moratorium was in a leaflet handed out at the Sydney demo against the ABC "ABC oppresses homosexuals" on 11 July 1973. It was mentioned as an example of how the media had ignored Gay Lib because GL presence was not mentioned in any of the reports of the Moratorium even though it was the first time they had marched.

33 Information for this section comes from *Sydney Gay Liberation Newsletter* no. 10, July 1973. Quotes from Jack Mundey in this section in http://www.australianbiography.gov.au/subjects/mundey/interview4.html; and Jeremy Fisher in his address at the launch of "Boas, boots 'n all: An exhibition tracing gay and lesbian trade union activism" in the auditorium of Unions NSW, 277 Sussex Street, Sydney NSW 2000 on 7 February 2007; "Gay student victimised", *Direct Action* no.43, 28 June 1973

34 Jeremy Fisher's case came up during university holidays making it difficult to organise student meetings, rallies, etc. As well as the rally outside the student union called a meeting for June 20 of students at affiliated residential colleges. A petition condemning Cole was an initiative from this meeting. By June 26 97 of the 200 residents had signed the petition. SRC Letter 26.6.73 M/C/J collection.

35 "Protests on student ban", *Tribune*, 2-8 April, 1974, p.12; "Teachers Fed with Penny Short", *Tribune*, 9-15 April, 1974, p.12; "BLF protest Penny Short", *Tribune*, 30 April-May 6, 1974, p.12; "Gay trainee teacher victimised", *Direct Action* no.59, 13.4.1974, p.9

36 In 1975 some groups representing blacks, women and gays and some other radical groups were banned by the May Day committee from joining the march. Union leaders physically attacked people from these groups when they joined the rally. Bob Hawke, as the report said "showing true colours, sneering and predatory, calling us fascist and saying we'd never had it so good." Queensland University *Campus Camp Newsletter* no.4 May 1975

37 Johnston, 1973, pp.2-3 Johnston was one of the protesters.

38 Gay Liberation Manifesto (1973). There were two Manifestos – one from the USA which was reprinted in CAMP Ink *William and John* 1(4) 6-11. June-2 Aug 1972. A second, more radical one from the London GLF which was reprinted with some added references to Australia in *Gay Rays* 1972 and in the 1973 Gay Pride Week broadsheet, 8-16.9.1973

39 Gowland, 1973, p.8. Sydney Gay Lib papers (ALGA) Program for the conference.

40 *Sydney Gay Liberation Newsletter* Vol.1, no.7 January 1973

41 *Sydney Gay Liberation Newsletter* Vol 1, no. 9 July 1973.
42 See *Sydney Gay Liberation Newsletter* no.10 July 1973, p.1 "Gay Pride Week"
43 ibid
44 Johnston, 1999. The psychiatrist was Harry Bailey.
45 "Sydney Gay Pride Demo" by Di Minnis and "Melbourne: Gay Pride week reviewed" – both in *Melbourne Gay Liberation Newsletter*, no.5, October 1973
46 "Militant Gay Lib march". *Tribune* 18.9.1973 p.8. BLF members on a nearby jobsite took the protesters' side, tossing a bucket of water on the cops – unfortunately not stopping the arrests. Later, workers from the job put up a fair bit of the bail money, alongside the CPA and Macquarie University Student Council. *Direct Action* 27.9.1973 pp.8-9.
47 Ciszak, 2006, p.26
48 Melbourne Gay Liberation nd – c.1982,
49 Pam Stein "Women's Oppression" *Sydney Gay Liberation Newsletter* Vol 1 no. 6, December 1972
50 "Woman Identified Woman" at http://library.duke.edu/rubenstein/scriptorium/wlm/womid/womid-p1-72.jpeg 1970; Radical Lesbian Conference, Sorrento, July 1973 http://users.spin.net.au/~deniset/alesfem/s1sitka.pdf
51 Lesbian Feminist Conference *Tribune* 27 November 1973, p.11
52 Mercer, p.442
53 C Johnston and Michael Hurley "Campfires of Resistance" First National Homosexual Conference, 1975 Papers, p.23

Chapter 5

1 Rosas, 1975. Rosas joined the Communist Party, then the SWP before joining the Spartacist League.
2 Johnston and McGahen, 1974
3 Gowland, 1975 p.16
4 Willett, 2000, pp.90-91
5 All quotes from Phil Carswell from interviews with Graham Willett in 1996 and Liz Ross in 2012.
6 Phil Carswell notes that this was the first ever Homosexual Caucus at AUS and caused somewhat of a stir. It was a "coming out" for some, the first time they'd publicly acknowledged being gay.
7 The *Zap!* leaflet was signed by 19 people: Laurie Bebbington, Bob Cotter, Phillip Carswell, Jeff Hayler, Margaret Lyons, Tasma Ockenden, Ian Malloy, Brian Pola, Helen Lang, Chris Lee, Ron Thiele, Stuart Macdonald, Steven Barca, Helen Golding, Bruce James, Peter O'Connor, Craig Johnston, Larry

Endnotes

Perry, Gay Walsh. Five of the signatories – Bebbington, Carswell, Hayler, Lyons and Thiele – were to be members of the Conference Organizing Committee of the first National Homosexual Conference.

8   The motions were put forward by Ian Malloy, a delegate from Footscray Institute of Technology, and Brian Pola, a member of the national executive. They were carried.

9   SWP leaflet; *Hard Lines* Rev Comms leaflet; CPA leaflet May 1975.

10 *Lots Wife*. At La Trobe, the CPA(ML) rejected the AUS motions and put a counter position to adopt" a policy of opposing the legal and especially, the social persecution of homosexuals". They also argued that Gay Liberation was a "product of US imperialist cultural penetration into Australia and that it fulfilled a function, in those countries which are oppressed by US imperialism, of diverting, confusing and splitting on unnecessary grounds the respective national liberation movements." Barry York *National U*, 9.6.75. At Monash Albert Langer said the Maoists did not support the persecution of gays. Tom O'Lincoln. Personal Communication 22.1.2013.

11 *Gay Teachers and Students Newsletter*, 1975-1980

12 Davis, 1975 pp.36-38; Wilson, 1975. pp.79-85

13 Bebbington and Lyons, 1975 pp.47-48

14 Authors of these papers were Peter Hawkins, Craig Johnston and Michael Hurley and Angelo Rosas

15 *Lesbian Newsletter* no, 13 1978

16 It is signed by Vaughan (Hinton); Lance Gowland; Craig Johnston, Peter Murphy, Jeff McCarthy, Angelo Rosas. *Red and Lavender* no.1, 6 December 1976; The Manifesto broadsheet was published as part of *Lots Wife* 2 August 1976, pp15-18

17 *Red and Lavender* no.5, 18 March 1977

18 In 1974 Lance Gowland, then a member of the union, interviewed B Bolger the NSW State Secretary of the Waterside Workers Federation (now MUA). Bolger showed a complete disregard for both gay and women's rights, though was, justifiably, proud of the union's stance on Indigenous rights. The union did change its stance and there is an early example of it supporting one its members, a drag queen, on the wharves. *Camp Ink*, Vol 4, no.2 December 1974 pp.3-4; In 1979 the Victorian Gay Trade Unionist Group (VTUG) reported that the Waterside Workers Federation pledged 100% support for any victimised member and that the union Executive was considering affiliation with VTUG. VTUG Minutes 11.6.1979.

19 *Melbourne Truth* 16 December 1972 p.32

20 Ostenfeld, 1996, p.201. The policy changes were adopted via the ACTU's Working Women's Charter which came out of the Working Women's Centre. The centre was established in 1975 with a grant from the Whitlam government and was headed by Sylvie Shaw, also a member of the CPA.

21 "Coming out at work" *Camp Ink* April 1972, p.13. The article was republished from August 1971 *Gay Sunshine*..

22 *Red and Lavender* no.7 September 1977
23 As quoted in "Free Speech threatened for gays" Brett Trenery *Direct Action* 8.11.73
24 *Red and Lavender* no.7 September 1977
25 Bebbington quoted in "Gay workers group forms in Melbourne", *Campaign*, no. 38 November 1978.
26 "Plumbers adopt anti-discrimination policy." Alan Hough *Gay Community News* Vol. 2 no.3 March 1980
27 Bill Leslie interview
28 *Red and Lavender* no.3, 1 February 1977; no.4, 8 March 1977
29 *Courier Mail* 5 September 1984
30 *Red and Lavender* no. 9 January 1978; Greg Weir Defence Newsletters; Greg Weir Profile: Oppose victimisation of a homosexual teacher. AUS 1977
31 "Let Greg Weir teach", *Camp Ink* no. 40, March 1977, p.12
32 Report on the Conference Don Baxter, *Gay Changes* Vol 2, no.2, Summer 1978
33 It included Tramways, Railways, Vehicle Builders, Waterfront workers, the Electricians and Miscellaneous Workers Union Liquor Trades (now Unite). Government clerical workers, Social Welfare, Theatrical unions also took a stand.
34 "Union makes stand for gay rights". *The Gay Trade Unionist* no.9 Oct-Nov 1979
35 Ostenfeld,. 1999, pp.157-190
36 *Young Gay and Proud* was produced by the Melbourne Gay Teachers and Student group. They'd hoped to get it circulating through schools via sympathetic teachers. While some managed to get it into school libraries the conservative government soon got wind of it and banned it from schools.
37 *Sydney Gay Liberation Newsletter* September 1977; *Sydney Gay Liberation Newsletter* no.9, January 1978
38 Carbery, 1995, p.11; The following account comes from Carbery and the many reports in the mainstream, gay and left-wing media.
39 Terry Goulden "The Gay Community: Who speaks for us?" *klick!* December 1980, p.34
40 O'Lincoln, 2009
41 Johnston, 1999, pp.100-110; p. 80

The Battle of Ideas
1 Anonymous
2 William and John Vol1 no.7, 1972, p.64

Endnotes

3 *Scarlet Woman* October-November 1977 no.6.
4 Heidi Hartmann's *The unhappy marriage of Marxism and Feminism* is the most famous of these attempts. Liz Jacka interview *Scarlet Woman* no.6, October-November 1977
5 Bloodworth, 2006 pp1-2.
6 Johnston, 1999 pp.82-83
7 Chris Sitka in Angelides, 2000 p.125. One of the more reactionary manifestations of this was a group in the US, founded by Valerie Solanas called SCUM – the Society for Cutting Up Men.
8 Johnston, 1999 p. 82
9 *Lesbian Newsletter* (Melbourne) October 1980
10 Hartmann, 1979
11 Stone, J, 1978; Bloodworth, 2006.

Chapter 6

1 GLF leaflet "Gay Liberation Front" 1972
2 See also Willett, 1996-7. See O'Lincoln, 2012, pp,12-13 for a discussion of the 'new middle class' and its make up.
3 Johnston, 1999, p.29.
4 Dennis Altman experienced this when he was lecturing in 1973. Expecting that his students were middle-class, he discovered that most were from Western Sydney with parents who were factory workers. "Discussions with Dennis Altman". *Overland* no.55 Winter 1973 pp.35-42
5 Burgmann, 1993 p.6,7
6 Symons and Cahill, 2005.
7 Ken Davis in *A Turbulent Decade*, 2005 pp.43-46; these quotes p.45; Ken Davis. Interview
8 Phil Carswell interview with Graham Willett.
9 In October 1979 the Victorian Gay Trade Unionist Group sent a letter to the SPA requesting information on party's attitude homosexuality. Their reply was: "So far the Socialist Party has not determined a policy on this question, nor have we published any articles in *The Socialist* or elsewhere relating to it..." The SPA became the Communist Party when the original CPA dissolved itself in 1991 and it now has a statement on its webpage supporting gay rights, though its coverage of gay issues is sparse.
10 Freney, 1991 pp.329-333
11 All quotes from Peter Murphy in this chapter come from an interview with the author.

133

12   Kate Davison 2007, p.60; second quote pp.63-64. There certainly appear to have been differences between the branches, with the Victorian branch and its publication *The Guardian* taking a much more Stalinist position on questions of sex and sexuality.
13   Ibid p.54
14   Peter Murphy. Interview; "Gay and lesbian existence under socialism. 'Pink love under the red star' Gay Laboratory Leningrad speak out" *Tribune* 26.6.1985 p.8-9
15   Bill Leslie. Interview
16   See O'Lincoln, 2009, for the ambiguities of the party's political evolution from the sixties onwards.
17   Freney, 1991 pp.329-333
18   Ibid p.261. Both these women were frequently mentioned in interviews with CPA members.
19   "Marxism and Gay Liberation – a personal viewpoint'. Brian McGahen. April 1978.
20   Gowland Pride History Group interview. *Sydney Gay Liberation Newsletter* July 1973.
21   ibid
22   Denis Freney "Aarons balls-up" *Sydney Gay Liberation Newsletter* vol 1 #8, Feb-May 1973. Freney was responding to an article about Mark Aarons and his homophobic attacks on student activist Jeff Hayler, *National U* 19.3.1973. *Camp Ink* 3, no.1 February 1973 p. 8
23   Denis Freney "Are homosexuals oppressed?" *Tribune* 11.9.1973 p.8.
24   Resolutions of the CPA 24th National Conference, 1974.
25   The following section on how the CPA organised around gay issues relies on information from interviews with Peter Murphy and Phil Carswell.
26   Gay Collective report to 1981 State Conference, NSW.
27   Collective Statement of Communist Party Gays to the Socialism and Homosexuality Conference, April 1981; Lesley Podesta Reply to CPA's "Collective Statement" to Socialism and Homosexuality Conference. 24 April 1981. Papers held at ALGA
28   Gaywaves interview. Held by Pride History Group, Sydney.
29   [31] ibid
30   Draft document for CPA 26th Congress, 1980. "What is this document for?" C Johnston *ALR* no.75, p.80
31   Johnston, 1999 pp.82-83
32   ibid
33   Freney, 1974, pp.16-18
34   Freney, 1991 pp.381-2; O'Lincoln, 2009

Endnotes

35 For simplicity I will refer to the various incarnations of the SWP and Resistance as the SWP. The youth group went by the name of SCREW (Sydney Committee for Revolution and Emancipation of the Working Class) for its first six months before changing its name to Resistance and then later to the Socialist Youth Alliance (SYA). Resistance itself also gave rise to the SWL. In 1978 SWL fused with the smaller Communist League to become the SWP. The paper began as *Direct Action* and became *Green Left Weekly* in 1991. The group changed its name to the Democratic Socialist Party and after various realignments is now known as the Socialist Alliance. A smaller group, the Revolutionary Socialist Party, resulted from a split in 2008 and is in a fusion process with Socialist Alternative.

36 Percy, 2005 p.50

37 ibid p.55

38 As were gay activists in the CPA. The IS had a long-running critique of Cuba and also condemned the treatment of gays in Cuba. This issue blew up again during the HIV-AIDS crisis with the Cuban regime's quarantine policy.

39 Ibid p.49, 53-54

40 The US SWP retreated in its support for Gay Liberation and more generally from Trotskyism from around 1979. It influenced the Australian SWP which also went through a major political shift at this time, turning to industry, pulling out of a lot of movements and Latin America solidarity work, likewise breaking with Trotskyism.

41 Statement for First National Homosexual Conference. Authorised by 14 SWP members. August 1975.The group was still called the Socialist Workers League. See fn.46

42 Jill Joliffe, "Vanguard on homosexuality", *Direct Action* no.8 July 1971, p.15. Jenny Ferguson. "Homosexual Liberation", *Direct Action* no.10, September 1971 p. 14. Both articles carried graphics from the US. The CPA(ML) was targeted because of its active homophobia on the campuses and because at Monash and LaTrobe they were a serious force on the left and a rival to the SWP.

43 There were 57 articles in 1978 with the numbers rapidly declining to 4 in 1980. The CPA's *Tribune* charted a similar result, though their numbers remained high till 1980 and then they rapidly declined with a low point of 2 in 1982. There were to be further highpoints in the 1990s with HIV-AIDS activism especially as well as "Queer" politics and then in the 2000s with the Equal Love-Gay Marriage rallies.

44 Memorandum on the Gay Liberation Movement . Adopted by the SYA National Committee at its October 13-14 plenum. (1973); Adopted by the SWL Political Committee on October 20, 1973

45 It is widely recognised that the day's events would not have happened without Ken Davis and others in the SWP and CPA.

46 The 1975 document "The socialist attitude to the homosexual struggle" was signed by 14 lesbian and gay SWP members, three in Melbourne, six

in Sydney and five in Adelaide. By 1978 there were around 48 members and supporters at an SWP caucus at the Fourth National Homosexual Conference. See fn.41

47 "1978 SWP GL report" *SWP Party Organiser* Vol.1, no.7. August 1978.
48 The hotel was closed down by the owners, Tooths' Breweries. It included a gay bar. There was a riot of about 4000 on the night it closed down. http://www.smh.com.au/articles/2004/09/16/1095320899843.html
49 SWP 7th National Conference. Strategy for homosexual liberation", *Direct Action*, 22 February, 1979, p.7
50 Both the attacks on gays in the US, UK and Canada and the right-wing agenda of the Fraser government were seen as laying the basis for a right-wing backlash in Australia.
51 "Strategy for homosexual liberation"
52 Tess Lee Ack, Janey Stone and Tom O'Lincoln interviews. All quotes in this section, unless otherwise attributed come from those interviews. Other information in this section comes from IS National Committee records.
53 The group was called the Marxist Workers Group and Socialist Workers Action Group (SWAG) before it became known as the IS. It has had two splits since then. One in 1985 to form Socialist Action, which re-merged with the original IS in 1990. The group then became known as the International Socialist Organisation. It split again in 1995 forming Socialist Alternative. While SA continues, the ISO has merged with other groups to form Solidarity. For histories of the IS and Socialist Alternative see: http://redsites.alphalink.com.au/ishistory.htm and http://marxistleftreview.org/index.php?option=com_content&view=article&id=77:the-origins-of-socialist-alternative-summing-up-the-debate&catid=34:issue-1-spring-2010&Itemid=77
54 See also *Lots Wife* for this period.
55 Left wing scientist and lecturer at Monash, Lesley Rogers, played an important role at Monash. She later ran the course through the Council for Adult Education. Rogers has written many important papers and books against biological determinism and other right-wing ideas about human behaviour. She was active in the campaign against racist right-wing scientists such as Hans Eysenck and Arthur Jensen.
56 *The Battler*. Vol 1 #1 November 17, 1972 p.6
57 The Homosexual Open Sub-committee was formed in 1976.
58 "Controversy: Which way forward for Australian gays" *International Socialist*, no.12, Summer 1981-82, pp.3-7
59 One indication that this stance (i.e. not autonomist) did not hinder friendly relations between I.S. and Gay Liberation in the early 1970s was a football match between the two groups.
60 Thorne no longer holds this position. She left the IS in the 1980s and joined The Freedom Socialist Party which supports autonomous organising.
61 Minnis left the IS soon after and no longer shares the group's politics.

62　Statement on socialists and the Gay Liberation Movement. Collected papers for the Socialism and Homosexuality Conference, 25-26 April 1981.

Chapter 7
1　Sydney Gay Liberation. Leaflet n.d (c.1972)
2　See also Jeffrey Weeks. English copies of Bernstein's articles in Die Neue Zeit have been posted at: http://www.studiesinanti-capitalism.net/StudiesInAnti-Capitalism/BERNSTEIN.html
3　"Statement on Socialist and the Gay Liberation Movement" IS Melbourne Gay Fraction. 1981 (For Socialism and Homosexuality Conference 25-26 April 1981)
4　http://www.generationonfire.com/fouratt.html

BIBLIOGRAPHY

All Australian lesbian and gay (or gay related) journals, newsletters, leaflets, theses, articles and many of the books, articles and other ephemera cited here, are held at the Australian Lesbian and Gay Archives [ALGA].

Newspapers, Journals, Newsletters

Australasian Lesbian Movement. Newsletter
Australian Left Review
The Battler (Paper of the International Socialists)
CAMP Ink
Campaign
The Communist (First paper of the Communist Party of Australia)
Direct Action (Paper of the Socialist Workers Party)
Gay and Lesbian Perspectives
Gay Community News
Gay Liberation Newsletter. Sydney
Gay Liberation Newsletter. Melbourne
Hard Lines (Newsletter of Revolutionary Communist Club Monash University)

Lesbian Newsletter. Melbourne

Lots Wife (Monash Student Newspaper)

The Socialist (Paper of the Victorian Socialist Party 1905-1923)

Tribune (Paper of the Communist Party of Australia. Successor to *Workers Weekly*)

William and John

Women's Liberation Newsletter. Melbourne

Women's Liberation Newsletter. Sydney

Workers Weekly (Paper of the Communist Party of Australia. Successor to *The Communist*)

Interviews

[All interviews except Tess Lee Ack, Tom O'Lincoln, Janey Stone and John Ware held at ALGA]

Rod Anderson (with author)

Phil Carswell (with author)

Phil Carswell (with Graham Willett)

Francesca Curtis (with author, Gary Jaynes and Graham Willett)

Ken Davis (with author)

Lance Gowland (at Pride History Group, Sydney)

Tess Lee Ack (with author)

Bill Leslie (with author)

Peter Murphy (with author)

Tom O'Lincoln (with author)

Phyllis Papps (with author, Gary Jaynes and Graham Willett)

Janey Stone (with Tom O'Lincoln)

John Ware Interview with Sara Dowse. 24.10.2010. http://nla.gov.au/nla.oh-vn5012690

Ephemera

Johnston/Minnis/Carswell, 1968-1980 Collection. A collection of key documents organised by Craig Johnston, Di Minnis and Phil Carswell for a projected, but never produced, history of Gay Liberation. Held at ALGA.

Books

Altman, Dennis *Homosexual. Oppression and Liberation.* Sydney, Angus & Robertson, 1972

Altman, Dennis *Coming out in the Seventies*, Sydney, Wild and Woolley, 1979

Bibliography

Anderson, Roderic *Free Radical. A memoir of a gay political activist.* Self published. 2006

Arrow, Michelle *Upstaged. Australian women dramatists in the limelight at last.* Sydney, Currency Press, 2002

Bernstein, Eduard and W Herzen Bernstein on homosexuality. Articles from *Die Neue Zeit* 1895 and 1898. Athol Books, 1977

Blasius, Mark and Shane Phelan, Eds *We are everywhere. A historical sourcebook of gay and lesbian politics.* NY Routledge, 1997

Blears, Barrie *Together with us. A personal glimpse of the Eureka Youth League and its origins. 1920 to 1970.* Sydney, Southwood Press, 2002

Bloodworth, Sandra *The poverty of patriarchy theory.* Melbourne, Socialist Alternative, 2006

Bongiorno, Frank *The sex lifes of Australians. A history.* Collingwood, Black Inc, 2012

Brown, Heather *A Marx on gender and the family. A critical study.* Leiden, Brill, 2012

Bullough, Vern Ed *Before Stonewall; Activists for Gay and Lesbian Rights in Historical Context.* NY, Haworth, 2002

Burgmann, Verity 'In our time'. *Socialism and the rise of Labor. 1885-1905.* Sydney, George Allen & Unwin, 1985

Burgmann, Verity *Power and Protest. Movements for change in Australian society.* Sydney, Allen & Unwin, 1993

Cant, Bob and Susan Hemmings. Eds *Radical records. Thirty years of lesbian and gay history.* London, Routledge, 1988

Carbery, Graham *Mardi Gras: a history of Sydney Gay and Lesbian Mardi Gras.* Melbourne, ALGA, 1995

Carleton, Gregory *Sexual revolution in Bolshevik Russia.* Pittsburgh, University of Pittsburgh Press, 2005.

Carter, David *Stonewall: the riots that sparked the gay revolution.* NY, St Martin's Press, 2004

Chesser, Lucy *Parting with my sex. Cross-dressing, inversion and sexuality in Australian cultural life.* Sydney, Sydney University Press, 2008

Chudacoff, Howard *The age of the bachelor: creating an American sub-culture.* Princeton, Princeton University Press, 1999

Clarsen, Georgine *Eat my dust. Early women motorists.* Johns Hopkins University Press, 2008.

Curthoys, Ann and John Merritt, Eds. *Australia's First Cold War.* Vol 1 *Society, communism and culture.* Sydney, George Allen & Unwin, 1984

Curthoys, Ann and John Merritt Eds *Australia's first Cold War* Vol 2. *Better red than dead.* North Sydney, Allen and Unwin, 1986

Damousi, Joy *Women come rally. Socialism, communism and gender in Australia 1890-1955.* Oxford, Oxford University Press, 1994

Damousi, Joy and Marilyn Lake, Eds *Gender and war. Australians at war in the twentieth century.* Cambridge, Cambridge University Press, 1995

Edge, Simon *With friends like these. Marxism and gay politics.* London, Cassell, 1995

D'Emilio, John *Sexual politics, sexual communities. The making of a homosexual minority in the United States, 1940-1970.* Chicago, University of Chicago Press, 1983

Duberman, Martin *Stonewall* NY, Plume, 1994

Engels, Frederick. *Origin of the family, private property and the state.* New York, International Publishers, 1972

Evans, Sara *Personal Politics. The roots of Women's Liberation in the Civil Rights movement and the New Left.* NY, Vintage, 1980

Ferrier, Carole *Jean Devanny. Romantic revolutionary.* Melbourne, Melbourne University Press, 1999

Field, Nicola *Over the Rainbow: money, class and homophobia.* London, Pluto Press, 1995

French, Robert *Camping by the billabong.* Sydney, Blackwattle Press, 1993

Freney, Denis *A map of days.* Sydney, Heinemann, 1991

Gallo, Marcia M *Different daughters. A history of the Daughters of Bilitis and the rise of the lesbian rights movement.* NY, Carroll & Graf, 2006

Gay Left Collective, Eds. *Homosexuality: Power and Politics.* London, Allison and Busby, 1980

German, Lindsay *Material Girls. Women, men and work.* London, Bookmarks, 2007

Gerster, Robin and Jan Bassett. *Seizures of youth. 'The Sixties' and Australia.* Sth Yarra, Hyland House, 1991

Greenberg, David F *The construction of homosexuality.* Chicago, University of Chicago Press, 1988

Hall, Richard *Black Armband Days.* Sydney, Vintage, 1998

Hay, Harry *Radically Gay. Gay Liberation in the words of its founders.* Edited by Will Roscoe. Boston, Mass, Beacon Press, 1996.

Healey, Dan *Homosexual desire in revolutionary Russia. The regulation of sexual and gender dissent.* Chicago, University of Chicago Press, 2001.

Hekma, Gert, Harry Oosterhuis and James Steakley, Eds *Gay men and the sexual history of the political left.* New York, Harrington Park Press, 1995.

Hewett, Dorothy *Bobbin Up.* 40th Anniversary Edition, Carlton, The Vulgar Press, 1999

Hobsbawm, Eric J *Revolutionaries: contemporary essays.* London, Quartet, 1982

Hunt, Gerald, Ed *Labouring for rights. Unions and sexual diversity across nations.* Philadelphia, Temple University Press,1999

Jay, Karla and Allen Young, *Out of the closets: the voices of Gay Liberation* NY, Douglas, 1972

Bibliography

Johnson, David K *The Lavender Scare. The Cold War persecution of gays and lesbians in the federal government.* Chicago, University of Chicago Press, 2004

Johnston, Craig *A Sydney gaze. The making of gay liberation.* Glebe, Wild & Woolley, 1999

Kaplan, Gisela *The meagre harvest. The Australian women's movement, 1950s-1990s.* St Leonards, Allen & Unwin, 1996

Kaplan, Gisela and Lesley J Rogers *Gene worship. Moving beyond the nature/nurture debate over genes, brain and gender.* New York, Other Press, 2003

Kollontai, Alexandra *Selected articles and speeches.* New York, International Publishers, 1984

Kollontai, Alexandra. *Selected Writings.* Ed Alix Holt. London, Alison & Busby, 1977

Lake, Marilyn. *Getting Equal. The history of Australian feminism.* Sydney, Allen & Unwin, 1999

Lauritsen, John and David Thorstad *The early Homosexual Rights Movement.* Rev ed. New York, Times Change Press, 1995

Lee Ack, Tess *The Marxist tradition and women's liberation.* Melbourne, Socialist Alternative, 2005.

Macintyre, Stuart *The Reds. The Communist Party of Australia from origins to illegality.* St Leonards, Allen & Unwin, 1995

Marx, Karl, Frederick Engels, V I Lenin, Joseph Stalin. *The Woman Question. Selections from the writings.* New York, International Publishers, 1951

Moore, Clive *Sunshine and rainbows. The development of gay and lesbian culture in Queensland.* St Lucia, University of Queensland Press, 2001.

Moore, Nicole *The censor's library.* St Lucia, University of Queensland Press, 2012

Morgan, Pete Class in the gay community. London, Socialist Worker, 1998 (first published in *International Socialism* 78 Spring 1998)

Murphy, John *Imagining the Fifties. Private sentiment and political culture in Menzies' Australia.* Sydney, UNSW Press, 2000

Murphy, John and Judith Smart, Eds *The forgotten fifties. Aspects of Australian society and culture in the 1950s.* Melbourne, Melbourne University Press, 1997 [Special issue of Australian Historical Studies Vol 28, no.109, October 1997.]

O'Hanlon, Seamus and Tanja Luckins *Go! Melbourne in the sixties.* Beaconsfield, Circa, 2005

O'Lincoln, Tom *Into the Mainstream.* Melbourne, Red Rag, 2009.

O'Lincoln, Tom *Australia's Pacific war. Challenging a national myth.* Melbourne, Interventions, 2011

O'Lincoln, Tom *Years of Rage. Social conflicts in the Fraser era.* Melbourne, Intervention 2012.

Percy, John *Resistance: A history of the Democratic Socialist Party and Resistance.* Vol 1: 1965-72. Chippendale, Resistance Press, 2005.

Reynolds, Robert *From camp to queer. Re-making the Australian homosexual.* Carlton, Melbourne University Press, 2002

Robinson, Shirleene Ed *Homophobia. An Australian history.* Sydney, The Federation Press, 2009

Rogers, Lesley *Sexing the Brain* London, Weidenfeld & Nicolson, 1999

Steakley, James *The homosexual emancipation movement in Germany.* Salem, Ayer, 1993 (1975).

Stein, Marc *City of Sisterly and Brotherly Loves: Lesbian and Gay Philadelphia.* Chicago, Chicago University Press, 2000

Stevens, Joyce *Taking the revolution home. Work among women in the Communist Party of Australia.* Melbourne, Sybylla Press, 1987

Stone, Hannah and Abraham *A marriage manual: A practical guide to sex and marriage.* Sydney, Halstead Press, 1945

Stone, Janey *Perspectives for Women's Liberation. Radical feminism, reform or revolution?* Melbourne, Redback Press, 1978

Symons, Beverley and Rowan Cahill, Eds *A turbulent decade. Social protest movements and the labour movement, 1965-1975.* Sydney, ASSLH, 2005

Tamagne, Florence. *A history of homosexuality in Europe. Berlin, London, Paris, 1919-1939.* 2 vols. New York, Algora, 2004

Teal, Donn *The gay militants* NY, Stein and Day, 1971

Thompson, Denise *Flaws in the social fabric. Homosexuals and society in Sydney.* Sydney, George Allen & Unwin, 1985

Timmons, Stuart *The trouble with Harry Hay. Founder of the modern gay movement. A biography.* Boston, Alyson, 1990

Walter, Aubrey Ed *Come together – the years of gay liberation 1970-73.* London, Gay Men's Press, 1980

Weeks, Jeffrey. *Coming Out: Homosexual Politics in Britain, from the Nineteenth Century to the Present.* London, Quartet, 1977.

Willett, Graham *From camp to gay: the homosexual history of the University of Melbourne, 1960-1976.* Melbourne University History Unit, Working Paper no.6. 2002

Willett, Graham. *Living Out Loud: A History of Gay and Lesbian Activism in Australia.* Sydney, Allen & Unwin, 2000

Willett, Graham, Daniel Marshall and Wayne Murdoch, Eds *The secret history of Queer Melbourne.* Melbourne, ALGA, 2011

Wilson, Colin *Socialists and gay liberation.* SW (UK) 1994

Wolf, Sherry *Sexuality and socialism. History, politics and theory of LGBT liberation.* Chicago, Haymarket, 2009

Wotherspoon, Garry *City of the plain. History of a gay sub-culture.* Sydney, Hale & Iremonger, 1991

Bibliography

Articles, Book Chapters and Theses

Allen, Judith "Marxism and the man question: some implications of the patriarchy debate." pp.91-111 In Judith Allen and Paul Patton, Eds *Beyond Marxism? Interventions after Marx*, Intervention Publications, 1983

Alomes, Stephen, et al "The social context of postwar conservatism", pp.1-28, in Curthoys and Merritt, Eds. *Australia's First Cold War. Vol 1 Society, communism and culture*. Sydney, George Allen & Unwin, 1984

Altman, Dennis "gay liberation", *Tharunka* 28 July 1971, p.11

Altman, Dennis "The emergence of gay identity in the USA and Australia", pp.30-55. In Christine Jennett and Randal G Stewart, Eds, *Politics of the future. The role of social movements*. Sth Melbourne, Macmillan, 1989

Angelides, Steven Gay Liberation and the paradox of bisexuality. *Gay &Lesbian Perspectives*, no.5, 2000 pp.113-131

Bebbington, Laurie and Jocelyn Clarke "Lesbian oppression and liberation". pp.59-61 National Women's Conference on Feminism and Socialism. Papers Melbourne October 1974

Bebbington, Laurie and Marg Lyons "Why SHOULD we work with you? Lesbian-Feminists versus 'gay' men." pp.47-8, First National Homosexual Conference, Melbourne. Papers 1975

Bell, Terence "A History of Sydney Gay Liberation". 1975

Bloodworth, Sandra "Marx and Engels on gender and sexuality and their legacy". *Marxist Left Review*, Melbourne, no 1, August 2010, pp.65-109

Carbery, Graham "Towards homosexual equality in Australia". *The La Trobe Journal*, no.87 May 2011, pp.164-166

Chesser, Lucy *Negotiating subjectivities: the construction of lesbian identities in Melbourne, 1960-1969*. University of Melbourne, Honours Thesis 1993

Ciszek, Derek M *Stonewall: the making of a transnational icon and Australian Gay Liberation, 1969-79*. Unpublished thesis, 2006

Cowan, Malcolm 'Knowing' Sodom? Australian churches and homosexuality. *Gay and Lesbian Perspectives* No.3, 1996 pp.207-239

Cowan, Malcolm and Tim Reeves "The 'Gay Rights' Movement and the decriminalisation debate in South Australia, 1973-1975. *Gay and Lesbian Perspectives* no. 4, 1998 pp.164-193

Cranenburgh, Naomi *From Invisible to 'Menace': Lesbians in Australia from 1939 to 1965*. Unpublished thesis. Monash University 2010

Davis, Ken "Capitalism and homosexual oppression." pp.36-8 First National Homosexual Conference, Melbourne. Papers 1975.

Davison, Kate *Pinks under the bed. Homosexuality, communism and nationalist sentiment in Cold War Australia*. University of Melbourne. Honours Thesis. May 2005.

Draper, Hal Marx and Engels on Women's Liberation. *ISJ* (1st series) 44 July/August 1970 pp.20-29. http://www.marxists.org/archive/draper/1970/07/women.htm

Engels, Frederick The book of Revelations. From Marx and Engels on religion. Progress Press 1957. [Written 1883] Accessed at: http://www.marxists.org/archive/marx/works/subject/religion/book-revelations.htm

Ferres, Kat "Written on the body: Jean Devanny, sexuality and censorship." *Hecate* Vol 20, no.1 1994

Fisher, Jeremy "Pink Bans: The historic role of the New South Wales Builders' Labourers' Federation in support of gay rights". 2007

Fogarty, Walter J "'Certain habits': The development of a concept of the male homosexual in New South Wales law, 1788-1900." *Gay Perspectives* no.1, 1992 pp.59-76

Ford, Ruth "Speculating on Scrapbooks, Sex And Desire: Issues in Lesbian History" *Australian History Studies* no. 106, 1996.

Ford, Ruth "'And merrily rang the bells': Gender-Crossing and same-sex marriage in Australia, 1900-1940." *Gay and Lesbian Perspectives* no.5, 2000, pp.41-66.

Foss, Paul "Gay Liberation in Australia" *William and John* Vol 1, no.8 1973 pp.5-9, 72;

French, Robert "'Where the action was': Archival sources for gay history in Australia." *Gay Perspectives* no.1 1992 pp.181-195

Freney, Denis "Comments on Gay Liberation", *GLP* August 1974, pp.16-18

Gays and Lesbian Aboriginal Alliance "Peopling the empty mirror. The prospects for lesbian and gay Aboriginal history". Gay Perspectives, no.2, 1994, pp.1-62

Gowland, Lance "Gay Lib Camp" *Tribune* 30 January 1973 p.8

Gowland, Lance "Strategy for the gay movement." *Camp Ink* Vol.4, no.3&4 April 1975 p.16

Griffiths, Phil Women and the CPA: 1920-1945. 1998 http://www.philgriffiths.id.au/writings/Aust_hist_old.html

Grosz, Elizabeth and Mia Campioni "Marxism and feminism." In Judith Allen and Paul Patton, Eds *Beyond Marxism? Interventions after Marx*, Intervention Pubns. 1983

Hartmann, Heidi "The unhappy marriage of Marxism and feminism: towards a more progressive union." *Capital & Class* Vol 3, no. 2, 1979 pp.1-33

Hobart Women's Action Group "Sexism and the Women's Liberation Movement. Or why straight women sometimes cry when they are called lesbians" *Camp Ink* Vol 3, no. 2 March 1973 pp.8-12.

Hodge, Dino "The okayness of gayness. Don Dunstan's record in homosexual law reform." *Gay and Lesbian Perspectives* no.6, 2011, pp.36-55

Hurley, Michael "Aspects of gay and lesbian life in seventies Melbourne." *The La Trobe Journal*, no.87 May 2011, pp.44-59

Bibliography

Koedt, Anne *Loving another woman*. 1973 (leaflet nd)

Johnston, Craig "May Day massacre" by *Sydney Gay Liberation Newsletter* no.9 July 1973 pp.2-3.

Johnston, Craig "Civil disobedience by the gay and lesbian movements: fashion, media, glamor? (notes from an investigation, or an archeology of tactics)." Australian Homosexual Histories conference, 2, 19 November 1999

Johnston, Craig "Radical Homosexual Politics: Into the Eighties. Part I" *Gay Information*, no.2, May-June 1980, pp.8-12

Johnston, Craig "Radical Homosexual Politics: Into the Eighties. Part II." *Gay Information* no.3 August-September 1980, pp.8-11

Johnston, Craig and Robert Johnston "The making of homosexual men" pp.87-99. In Verity Burgmann and Jenny Lee, eds, *Staining the Wattle. A people's history of Australia since 1788*. Ringwood, Penguin, 1988

Johnston, Craig and Brian McGahen "Draft statement of revolutionary homosexuals on the GLF". 15.2.1974 (Leaflet M/C/J Collection)

Lee, John et al "Toward a workable Sydney Gay Liberation" *Sydney Gay Liberation Newsletter*, 1972

Lee, John "Male homosexual identity and subculture in Adelaide before World War II." *Gay Perspectives* No.1, 1992, pp.95-112

Melbourne Radicalesbians "The Melbourne Gay Women's Group", pp.441-445. In Mercer, Jan Ed. *The other half. Women in Australian society*. Middlesex, Penguin, 1975

Mimichild, Christine "Gay & straight in the movement." *The Ladder*, Apr/May72, Vol. 16 Issue 7/8, p.23-26

Moore, Clive "Pink Elephants and drunken police: bohemian Brisbane in the 1940s." *Gay and Lesbian Perspectives* No. 1V, 1998, pp.132-163

Moore, Clive "Coming out ready or not: gay liberation politics in Queensland 1970s-1980s." *Gay and Lesbian Perspectives* #5, 2000, pp.85-98

Morgain, Rachel Sexual liberation: fighting lesbian and gay oppression. At: http://dspace.anu.edu.au/bitstream/1885/42704/1/Sexual_liberation.pdf

Morris, Meaghan "Male politics on May Day" *MeJane* Vol2, no.1, July 1973

Murdoch, Wayne "'Disgusting doings' and 'putrid practices'. Reporting homosexual men's lives in the Melbourne *Truth* during the First World War." *Gay and Lesbian Perspectives* No. 4 1998, pp.116-131

Ostenfeld, Shane "Interactive Movements: The Gay, Women's and student movements and the trade unions." *Gay and Lesbian Perspectives* no.3 1996 pp.189-206

Ostenfeld, Shane "Sexual identity and the Australian labor movement in historical perspective." pp.157-190. In Gerald Hunt, Ed *Labouring for rights. Unions and sexual diversity across nations*. Philadelphia, Temple University Press,1999

Parker, Clare and Paul Sendziuk "It's time. The Duncan case and the decriminalisation of homosexual acts in South Australia, 1972." *Gay and Lesbian Perspectives 6*, 2011 pp.17-35

Paxton, Nancy "From cosmopolitan romance to transnational fiction: re-reading Jean Devanny's Australian novels." pp.215-228. In Nancy L. Paxton in Desley Deacon, Penny Russell, Angela Woollacott Eds *Transitional Ties. Australian Lives in the World*. Canberra, ANU Press, 2008. http://epress.anu.edu.au/wp-content/uploads/2011/03/prelims3.pdf

Poll, Christobel "Gay Liberation" *Old Mole* 26.10.1970 no.7 p.5

Robinson, Lucy "Carnival of the Oppressed: The Angry Brigade and the Gay Liberation Front." *University of Sussex Journal of Contemporary History*, Issue Six, August 2003.

Rogers, Lesley "Biology and human behaviour", pp.33-48. In Mercer, Jan Ed. *The other half. Women in Australian society*. Middlesex, Penguin, 1975

Rogers, Lesley "On being a political lesbian", pp.104-115. In Margaret Bradstock and Louise Wakeling, Eds, *Words from the same heart*. Sydney, Hale & Iremonger, 1987

Rosas, Angelo "The intellectual history of Sydney Gay Liberation 1973-4." September,1975.

Ross, Liz *Marxism and homosexuality*. http://www.anu.edu.au/polsci/marx/gayleft/marxismandhomsexuality.htm.

Ross, Liz "Love's Coming of Age: Australian socialist and communist parties and sexuality". *The La Trobe Journal*, no. 87 May 2011, pp.107-115

Ross, Liz "We were catalysts for change." *Journal of Lesbian Studies*, vo. 13, no.4 October 2009, pp.442-460

Ross, Liz "Escaping the well of loneliness", pp.100-108. In Verity Burgmann and Jenny Lee, eds, *Staining the wattle. A people's history of Australia since 1788*. Ringwood, Penguin, 1988

Sargent, Dave "Reformulating (Homo) Sexual Politics: radical theory and practice in the gay movement." pp.163-183. In Judith Allen and Paul Patton, Eds *Beyond Marxism? Interventions after Marx*, Intervention Publications. 1983

Di Sciascio, Peter "Australian lesbian artists of the early twentieth century." *Gay and Lesbian Perspectives* no.6, 2011 pp.135-155.

Sitka, Chris "A Radicalesbian herstory" http://users.spin.net.au/~deniset/alesfem/slsitka.pdf

Smaal, Yorick "Friends and lovers. Social networks and homosexual life in war-time Queensland, 1938-1948." *Gay and Lesbian Perspectives* no.6, 2011 pp.168-187.

Stone, Janey "What is the party line on love?" *The Battler*, Vol 1, no. 1, p.6, 17 November 1972.

Stone, Janey "Who are we, where are we going?" *Vashti's Voice* no.1.1972

Widdup, David "The first year of the movement" nd (c.1976)

Bibliography

Willett, Graham "Foucault and the History of Homosexuality. A properly historical consideration." *Melbourne Historical Journal*, Vol. 24 pp.10-25 1996

Willett, Graham "Marxists and the gay movement."*Re-construction* no.9, Summer 1996-7 pp.25-31

Willett, Graham "The darkest decade: homophobia in 1950s Australia" pp.120-132 in John Murphy and Judith Smart, Eds, *The forgotten fifties. Aspects of Australian society and culture in the 1950s*. Melbourne, Melbourne University Press, 1997

Willett, Graham "Minorities can win: The gay movement, the left and the transformation of Australian society." *Overland* 149, 1997 pp.64-68.

Willett, Graham "Marxism and the new social movements: the case of gay liberation" pp.201-208 in Carole Ferrier, Rebecca Pelan, Eds *The Point of Change: Marxism/Australia/History/Theory*. UQP. 1998.

Willett, Graham "Anglicanism and homosexuality in the 1970s." pp.41-65 In: *People of the Past?: The Culture of Melbourne Anglicanism and Anglicanism in Melbourne's Culture*; Holden, Colin (Editor). Parkville, Vic.: University of Melbourne, Department of History. Melbourne University conference and seminar series:9, 2000

Willett, Graham "The origin of homosexual politics in Australia." *Gay and Lesbian Perspectives* no.5, 2000, pp.67-84.

Willett, Graham "Party like it's 1958" *MCV* no 22, 6 August 2008, p.53.

Willett, Graham "Moods of Love and Commitment: Laurence Collinson in Melbourne." *The La Trobe Journal*, no 83, May 2009 pp.77-90

Willett, Graham "From 'vice' to 'homosexuality': policing perversion in the 1950s". pp.113-127 in Shirleene Robinson, Ed, *Homophobia in Australian History*, Leichhardt, Federation Press, 2009

Willett, Graham "'We blew our trumpets and...' The ACT Homosexual Law Reform Society. Out Here." *Gay and Lesbian Perspectives* no.6, 2011, pp.1-16

Wills, Sue Wills "Inside the CWA: The Other One" *Journal of Australian Lesbian Feminist Studies* 4 1994, pp.6-22

Wills, Sue "The politics of sexual liberation" PhD Thesis, University of Sydney, 1981

Wilson, Richard "Political perspectives for an independent homosexual movement." pp.79-85. First National Homosexual Conference, Melbourne. Papers,1975

Wood, Katie "Fighting anti-union laws: the Clarrie O'Shea strikes", *Marxist Left Review* no.5, 2013, pp.105-131

Wotherspoon Gary "Gay Men in Sydney" *Sydney Journal* 2(1) June 2009, pp.39-49

www.ingramcontent.com/pod-product-compliance
Lightning Source LLC
Chambersburg PA
CBHW050315010526
44107CB00055B/2253